THE HISTORY OF *City Market*

THE HISTORY OF *City Market*

The BROTHERS FOUR *and the* COLORADO BACK SLOPE EMPIRE

ANTHONY F. PRINSTER AND KATE RULAND-THORNE

Published by The History Press
Charleston, SC 29403
www.historypress.net

First published 2013

Manufactured in the United States

ISBN 978.1.62619.286.7

Library of Congress CIP data applied for.

Notice: The information in this book is true and complete to the best of our knowledge. It is offered without guarantee on the part of the authors or The History Press. The authors and The History Press disclaim all liability in connection with the use of this book.

All views and opinions expressed in this book are those held by the authors and do not necessarily reflect the views or opinions of The Kroger Co., Dillon Companies Inc., or City Market.

This book is dedicated to the Prinster family—those who have gone before us, those who are with us now and future generations. This book is further dedicated to all City Market employees past and present, wherever they may be. They have always been a vital part of the City Market success. My hope is that this book records and preserves the City Market history for all to enjoy.

CONTENTS

PREFACE

The Continental Divide separates the state of Colorado into the Eastern Slope and the Western Slope. The Eastern Slope is also referred to as the "Front Range" and includes the Greater Denver Metropolitan Area. Over the years, friends and colleagues living on the Eastern Slope have, with good humor, referred to those of us from the Western Slope as "Back Slopers." We choose to wear this moniker as a badge of honor and distinction.

The Prinster family has lived on the Western Slope of Colorado for more than ninety years, yet until recently, little was known about our origins. Our family nurtured a small meat shop on North Fourth Street in Grand Junction, Colorado, and transformed the City Market brand into a retail grocery chain that dominated its market area for decades. As the great-grandson of Joseph, the grandson of Frank and the son of Frank Jr., I believed that the full story should be told—a story that begins with a penniless nineteen-year-old European immigrant and closes with the business becoming part of the largest supermarket chain in the United States. This book is my effort to do that.

Part of the hard work for me was to decide the scope and breadth of what should be covered during our 150-year history. Which of the fascinating events, people and documents that I found should be included? It had to be limited. I concluded that this story should stay focused on the City Market business and the specific family members who made it all happen between 1854 and 1970. It still wasn't easy.

Research for this book has been ongoing for more than ten years. I searched through the courthouse archives of Otero County in La Junta, Colorado, and those in Mesa County, Colorado. I traveled to Riffian, Italy, and also spent countless hours searching on the Internet. During that time, a statement attributed to Barbara Tuchman, the Pulitzer Prize–winning author of *The Guns of August*, came to mind. She proclaimed that doing historical research was seductively enjoyable, but the actual writing was hard work. She was right.

We have a large family. Family members live all around the United States and in several countries in Europe. There are people from all walks of life—nurses, teachers, engineers, computer scientists, writers, lawyers, soldiers, priests and monks. Each has an interesting story to tell and accomplishments to acknowledge. It would have been too difficult to tell everyone's story—that book would take a lifetime to write. In these pages (with the exception of a short chapter about the fifth brother, Edward the priest), the scope has been limited to the story of how a family business began and how it grew.

City Market began with an immigrant born in 1854, Josef Franz Pruenster. Little was known about his birthplace, his family, the place he came from and how he traveled. Searches of available ship passenger lists, census records and archived newspaper articles were often more confusing than helpful. Some believed that he immigrated from Hungary or Moravia, others Austria or Switzerland. His descendants believed that Austria or Switzerland was more likely. No one was ever sure. His immediate family remembered him talking of hiking near Innsbruck, his love of the mountains and how he longed to return there some day. He never did.

Over those years, our business touched the lives of many people in the food industry, family members, employees, friends and business associates. There were just too many to acknowledge individually. However, two very important groups must be recognized. City Market was successful not just because the Prinster family "worked like dogs" over four generations to make the business a success, but also because many individuals associated with the company in many different capacities contributed to its growth and success over the years. City Market had, as part of its essence, a core of very dedicated, loyal and hardworking employees. Those employees were major contributors to the ultimate success that City Market enjoyed; they helped make it an enterprise that survived hard times and the changes that City Market endured over the decades.

ACKNOWLEDGEMENTS

Work on this book began more than ten years ago with efforts to locate the path my great-grandfather followed from South Tyrol, Italy, to America. Credit for this end product, however, belongs to many creative, talented and hardworking individuals. Once started on this project, I found, without exception, that everyone who was asked to write, research or provide information was enthusiastically willing to help. That was a real treasure, and I thank everyone.

The writing team was first rate. My coauthor, Kate Ruland-Thorne, herself an accomplished author of many historical books, brought a colorful and creative style to the book that could never be found in dry old legal records and writings. She set the course and tone for telling the story. My brother, Thomas N. Prinster, provided two very important things: excellent creative writing advice and encouragement. Tom, I am grateful for your help. Our distant relative and my Internet friend Tayana Pruenster was a critical team member—simply put, a "gem." Tayana helped with historical information, documents, pictures and edits. To our delight, she proved herself to be an "editors' editor." Ann Griffin, my first cousin, was most helpful with her writing and knowledge of events in our grandparents' lives. George Orbanek was a welcome contributor as a "peer review" reader and editor. Margaret Allyson, of Dallas, Texas, another Internet friend, was masterful as our copy editor. Krystyn Hartman, of *Grand Valley Magazine*, gets the credit for finding many of the talented players and help in negotiating the path to the publishing world. Thank you, Krystyn.

Multiple hours were given in recorded interviews, which refreshed memories and helped to develop the factual historical data. These willing contributors were Joseph C. Prinster Sr., John H. Prinster, Lucille Haggerty, Miriam Peckham, Patricia "Penny" Prinster, Fran Higgins, Herb Bacon, Curtis Robinson and Don Lowman (vice-president, Otero Museum, La Junta, Colorado, who first told me about the "Zulu cars").

Documents, photographs and archived newspaper articles were provided courtesy of many sources: Dan Prinster and the Joseph C. Prinster family; the Woodruff Memorial Library staff and Heather Maes of La Junta, Colorado (they researched and found the newspaper articles from the *La Junta Tribune*, the *Daily Democrat* and the La Junta City Directory and Otero County Directories, as well as photographs); the Mesa County Libraries; the Museum of Western Colorado; City Market; Miriam Peckham; and Susan Cox and ABC Title and Closing Inc. of Ordway, Colorado. The work of Laurena Maynes Davis on the series of articles "The Journey," written for the City Market newsletter *Express Lines* in 1999, was also a great resource. Thanks to Mary Doring for her help in transcribing the interviews with Joseph C. Prinster.

A special thank-you to the Legends of the Grand Valley—a nonprofit organization committed to the preservation of the stories of those historically significant men and women who shaped Grand Junction, Colorado—for its support of the publication of this book.

To my wife, Sally L. Prinster: your valuable suggestions and unwavering support helped me through this project. Thank you.

PART I

THE IMMIGRANTS

THE PIONEER

There wasn't an empty pew in St. Patrick's Catholic Church in La Junta, Colorado, on the morning of November 25, 1929. It was a crisp autumn day, and the townspeople had gathered to mourn the passing of a beloved pioneer, J.F. Prinster, age seventy-five. Also in attendance were members of the Knights of Columbus, the Modern Woodmen and the Woodmen of the World. Mr. Prinster had been a member of all three organizations.

Seated in the first rows of the church were members of Mr. Prinster's family: his widow, Millie, four of his five living sons—Paul, Frank and Clarence and their families of Grand Junction and Edward of La Junta—daughter, Mary (Mrs. Donald Blevins), of Denver; and twelve grandchildren. Missing was his son Leo, who was too ill to attend. Other children were deceased: the youngest daughter, Lucille, who had died six years earlier at the age of sixteen, and sons Andrew, who had also passed at age sixteen, and Joseph, who did not survive infancy.

Following a solemn Requiem High Mass, twenty-one pallbearers accompanied Mr. Prinster's casket to the cemetery. All were not only good friends but also prominent members of the community, just as Mr. Prinster had been. When the procession left the church to go to the Calvary Cemetery, the mournful wail of a whistle from the Santa Fe Chieftain passing through La Junta sounded in the distance as if to pay a special tribute to one of its pioneers.[1]

Who was this man so revered by family, friends and an entire community? His family remembered him as a man who left them a legacy of virtues like endurance, loyalty, persistence, faith, a flair for innovation and the rewards of hard work. Everyone knew of his kindness and liked him. "He was good to poor people," they said. "He could not see anyone go hungry."[2] His life in La Junta was a model of industry and entrepreneurial spirit. These accolades were a deserving tribute to a life well lived and industry rewarded, but there was another Joseph Prinster, one who didn't quite match the paragon being offered. An immigrant to the United States, *that* Joseph (or rather, Josef) had kept secret his place of origin in Austria, as well as why he ran away from the old country at a very young age.[3]

His American family would have never dreamed on the day of the funeral what would happen more than half a century later.

A young woman from the village of Riffian in South Tyrol had been searching for her great-grandfather's long-lost brother, Josef Pruenster. Her name was Tayana Pruenster. All her life, she had heard the story of Josef, the only one in her family to leave for America and not return. Now, more than one hundred years after his departure, the family and community still talked about Josef. The idea of his journey stirred her imagination.

Tayana, fluent in several languages, loved to travel. When those travels took her to America, she examined phone books in whatever city she happened to be visiting in the hope of finding her ancestor's descendants. And one day, sixty-three years after Joseph's death, in a phone book in Tempe, Arizona, Tayana struck gold.

The letter, dated July 23, 1992, arrived at the winter home of Joseph C. Prinster in Tempe in early August of that year. It was a single typewritten page in English. It announced, "I am searching for my grandfather's uncle Mr. Prinster Joseph who moved to the city of La Junta in Colorado after 1900." It was postmarked "I–39010 Riffian (BZ) Italy," and signed Tayana Pruenster.[4] Letters were exchanged for the next few years.

Tayana was a twenty-three-year-old single woman who lived with her mother, Anna, and a younger sister, Jasmina, in a small apartment in the center of the village of Riffian, South Tyrol, Italy. When Anna's first daughter was born in 1969, Anna had liked the American hit song "Diana" performed by Paul Anka on his Italy tour in the late 1960s. Anna, with no grasp of English, heard the name as "Tayana" and gave her child that name.

Anna supported her daughters by working during the tourist season in a hotel located about two hundred meters from their small apartment. Anna's brother, Florian, and his family lived a short distance away on an old family farm called Obereggelehof. Florian had inherited the farm from his father, Anton, and remodeled it into a small hotel.[5]

Tayana wrote of the Pruenster family in Riffian, "They speak German as their mother tongue, or as they will tell you, a German dialect similar to the dialect in Bavaria, South Germany, when conversing. Their written correspondence is standard German."

South Tyrol had been part of Italy for only seventy-five years. It was made a separate district of Italy in 1919 after World War I.[6] In the schools, both Italian and German were taught. Tayana and her family, as well as most of the citizens of that area, are bilingual. In high school, English was a standard subject, so many spoke that language as well.

As a young girl, Tayana spent many hours with her grandmother, also named Anna. Tayana would be at her side as she went about the small hillside farm at Obereggelehof. As Grandmother Anna tended her flowers and fed the chickens, she spoke at length about the Pruenster family. She told how her husband, Anton Pruenster, had taken over the farm when his

Obereggelehof is the family home of Antonius Pruenster, youngest brother of Joseph Prinster. *Author's collection.*

father, Antonius, died in 1932. Anton worked hard to improve the farm. After Anna and Anton were married in 1941, he was drafted into the army, even though he had young children to support and should have been exempt from service. Anton was a foot soldier in the German army during World War II and suffered the savage and brutal conditions of the winter retreat from the Russian front. He returned home a scarred and changed man.

But the story Tayana remembered and liked the most was of her great-grandfather's brother Josef. Anna told her many times about Josef, who went to America and never returned. Josef was nine years older than Antonius and the middle son in the family of nine children. It was the law and tradition at that time that the oldest son inherited the paternal farm. This meant that neither Josef nor his younger brother, Antonius, would have the family farm, Ausserpircherhof. If they were to have a future, they had to build up something on their own or work for their oldest brother, Johann, as farmhands. The brothers, despite their age differences, talked at great length and pondered their choices and futures. Tayana's grandmother told how Antonius had worked many long and hard years as a farmhand to save money. When he had enough funds, he bought and built Obereggelehof in Riffian and operated it as a fruit-growing and cattle-breeding operation.

By that time, Josef had departed and was heard from infrequently, writing once or twice from some remote place in the American West. In about 1885, he wrote to his brother Antonius that he had reached La Junta, Colorado, and had changed his name from Pruenster to Prinster.[7] His first name, too, became Americanized as Joseph.

At one time in the early 1900s, he wrote to invite Antonius and their younger sister to follow him to the United States. Antonius declined the invitation because he didn't want to give up his new farm. He decided to remain in South Tyrol. He married in 1905 and had three sons; two died of illness during and after the Second World War, and the third son, Anton (Tayana's grandfather, born in 1907), took possession of Obereggelehof in 1932 and married Anna Frei in 1941.[8] Antonius and his wife also had twins in 1906, but they lived only ten days.

The story of Josef caught Tayana's imagination and stayed fixed in her memory. Of all the family over the centuries, he was the only one to leave and not return. As a young girl growing up, she had heard his story many times. Now, more than sixty-three years after his death, Joseph's American family would begin to learn the whole story of his life, thanks to Tayana.

Left: Anna Pruenster, Tayana's grandmother, was devoted to her family and their heritage. *Courtesy of Tayana Pruenster.*

Below: Antonius's family and friends in front of his farm, Obereggelehof, circa 1921. *Courtesy of Tayana Pruenster.*

JOSEF PRUENSTER: THE IMMIGRANT (1854–1873)

The area in South Tyrol where Josef Pruenster was born is known as *Passeiertal*, which means "area of the Passer River." The *Passeiertal* borders the *Vinschgau* near Switzerland and is cradled between Switzerland to the west and Austria to the north; it was controlled by the Hapsburgs until the end of World War I. The Passer River runs through a valley surrounded by craggy, snowcapped Alpine peaks of ten thousand feet, the most notable being the *Hirzer* to the east. The climate varies from Alpine zones to mid-temperate zones to a Mediterranean zone that supports palm trees in the towns and villages of the lower areas.

It is a lush and fertile mountainous farmland that produces a variety of fruits and vegetables, apples being the main crop, but also an abundance of pears, berries, grapes and strawberries. The lower valleys are populated with large estates producing wines of many varieties. In the mountains, livestock, milk production and farming are the main activities.

The farms are situated at elevations up to two thousand meters (6,500 feet), and the farmers work small tracts on extreme slopes, often grades of forty to forty-five degrees.[9] Walking through the slopes and fields, one can still see today the farmers wearing their traditional dark-blue Tyrolean work aprons as they toil in the fields and among the grapevines.

Mountain Range surrounding Riffian, South Tyrol, Italy. *Author's collection.*

The Passer River runs from the Alps through the Passer Valley through Meran, Italy. *Author's collection.*

The farms in the area date from the mid- to late thirteenth century. Ownership of real estate in those early times was kept in books at the local parish under the supervision of the parish priest. Records are still available but difficult to access.

Examination of the available real estate records shows a reference in AD 1357 to a farm owned by "Petrus the Pruenster." There is a record entry in AD 1394 to "Chunradan der Pruenste," which means "Konrad living on the farm Pruenster." The next entry found, "1553 AD Pruenst," is interpreted to mean "place of fire or place of burning." And there is an entry of "1694 *Pruenstguet*," which is believed to mean "land of the Pruenst."[10]

Josef Pruenster was born at Ausserpircherhof, a farm and house located in the small village of Vernuer about one mile from Riffian. To call Vernuer a village is an overstatement—a small hamlet might be a better characterization. Vernuer is mountainous; hayfields are on steep hillsides. In Josef's day, Vernuer was only accessible on foot from Riffian or by a cog railway, or "funicular," used to transport material and sometimes people. It was reported to be an adventurous experience to ride the funicular from the village of Riffian to the hamlet of Vernuer.

The hayfields in front of the family farm where Joseph Prinster was born. *Author's collection.*

Ausserpircherhof is a farmhouse perched at the top of a mountain slope and looks out on hayfields beneath the Passer River at the valley floor and the snow-covered Alpine peaks across the valley to the east. The records show that Josef's father bought the farm and the farmland in about 1840, before he was married.

The farmhouse is a two-story building of stone and wood timber construction. The family lived in the upper floor, which consisted of about five rooms. The milking pens, feed and hay and shelter for the livestock were on the lower floor. Ausserpircherhof was home to and the support of eleven people.

By the standards of its day, it must have been one of the larger and finer farm homes in the area. The surrounding farmland consisted of only about twenty acres, and the family owned about twenty-seven acres of woodland. Ample water from the nearby mountain ranges irrigated the hayfields. The acreage produced hay and grass to feed ten to fifteen cows. The family supported themselves by raising and breeding cattle, feeding them with the hay and grass in their meadows and selling their milk products such as cheese and butter. They also sold eggs from their chickens and timber from their forest. Until 1900, the family was self-catering. When they needed to buy something they couldn't produce themselves, they sold their products.

Ausserpircherhof was the birthplace of Josef Pruenster. *Author's collection.*

Josef's father was also named Josef Pruenster. He was born in January 1818. In 1847, he married Maria Gruener, a young woman from St. Leonhard, a nearby village, and they settled into Ausserpircherhof to raise their family. They had nine children: five girls and four boys. First came Maria, born in 1848. Anna was born in 1851 (she died in 1860). Johann, the eldest son, was born in 1852, and Josef, the second son, was born in 1854. After Josef, five more children were born: Theresia in 1856, another girl named Anna in 1860, Michael in 1863, Antonius in 1864 and Filomena in 1867.

After careful research and with the aid of a local teacher and historian, Renate Abram, Tayana pieced together an impression of Josef's school years in Riffian:

> *In 1774, Empress Maria Theresa introduced six years of compulsory education for boys in the empire, including in Southern Tyrol. The archives mention a "school mistress" as early as 1840. The school building of those days still stands today. It is next to the church in Riffian and is where my mother, aunt, and uncle went to school before the new building was finished in the 1950s. The children from Vernuer went to this school, which was a walk of at least one and a half hours each way. Walking a long way to school was not unusual for kids living in smaller villages here in South Tyrol until about 50 years ago. Boys, in particular, were required to attend school to the sixth grade. We can assume Josef had at least a sixth-grade education studying such subjects as mathematics, reading, writing, and religion. I think he acquired all the rest he needed for his journey, to live and survive in a very new place, in the school of life, with a very strong will to make his own way.*[11]

Primogeniture was the law or custom in most European sovereignties, including South Tyrol. The firstborn son would inherit the entire family estate to the exclusion of all other siblings. The brothers and sisters of the firstborn son had to find other paths to build their fortune. Their choices were few: stay with the eldest brother, working as farmhands or maids; the clergy; military service; or departure. To acquire their own assets was challenging, but it was not impossible. Johann, the eldest son, did inherit Ausserpircherhof and built it up over the course of his life. Josef's youngest brother, Antonius, toiled as a farmhand for years until he had funds saved to acquire land and build his own farm, Obereggelehof, on the outskirts of the village of Riffian. It operated as an agriculture enterprise growing fruit and

The Parrish Church of the Seven Sorrows of Mary, Riffian, Italy. *Author's collection.*

The onion-domed steeple is adjacent to the Parrish Church, which in 2010 celebrated seven hundred years as a pilgrimage church. *Author's collection.*

breeding and raising cattle. Both farms operate today and are owned by the descendants of Johann and Antonius.

But what of Josef? How did the world appear to him as a young man in mid- to late nineteenth-century Europe? He knew that there was no farm estate to inherit. He must have known that his most likely opportunity was as a day laborer, with only a very slight chance to get beyond that status. In those days, to travel beyond one's mountain-bound valley was rare. How could he gain exposure or find opportunities beyond the world of a little farm with eleven family members and fifteen dairy cows to support? Josef had never ventured outside his home valley. His skills were limited to what he had learned on the farm. He must have realized that his choices were bleak.

Josef was a citizen of the Austro-Hungarian monarchy and a subject of Emperor Franz Josef of Austria. The Austro-Hungarian empire was vast. It spread throughout Europe and parts of what are now Hungary and many other European countries. In 1868, when Josef was fourteen years old, the monarchy decreed a general conscription to the military. All young men of the realm, upon reaching their nineteenth birthdays, were required to serve in the KUK army (*kaiserlich und koeniglich*) for three years. In November 1873, Josef would turn nineteen and be required to enter military service in late 1873 or early 1874.[12] This compulsory service in the military was another choice for Josef. His service would have lasted until 1876, at which time he would have been twenty-two years old.

The army was not a pleasant career prospect, and records and memories indicate that Josef did not enter the military. Years later, among his American family, there was an understanding that Grandfather Joe "left Europe one step ahead of the Kaiser." Later, Joseph would tell his La Junta family that he did not want to have anything to do with the army or military service.

From about age eighteen, the trail of Josef Pruenster became a mystery to his European relatives. He left his family home and did not return. There are no known letters or correspondence from the time he could have been in military service. The only bit of firm information about Josef's youth is found in the files of his oldest daughter, Mary Prinster Blevins. In those files, there existed an unsigned and undated handwritten note that gives a clue to the decision Josef made about his future. "He ran away from home when he was very young."

Backstory Notes

As early as 15 BC, the Romans occupied the *Alpengebiet* (Alps region) of what today we know as South Tyrol. The area later fell into the hands of various warring German tribes. By AD 1258, it was under the control of Meinhard II, who is credited as being its founder. Meinhard II was count of Tyrol and gorizia and duke of Carinthia. He was a farsighted statesman and a shrewd politician, unscrupulous and ambitious. He created an autonomous area between the borders of Romanic and Germanic cultures. Under his rule, South Tyrol experienced an economic and cultural renaissance. Markets and towns were transformed into trading centers for goods. News and ideas filtered in from all over the world. Meinhard II's control and influence lasted until his death in 1295. Less than fifty years later, in 1363, Margarethe Maultasch, Meinhard's granddaughter, surrendered sovereignty of Tyrol to the Hapsburgs, who controlled it as part of the Austrian empire until 1867. The Austro-Hungarian empire existed between 1867 and 1918 at the end of World War I. The term "Suedtirol" (South Tyrol) exists only from 1918 to the present.[13]

JOSEPH PRINSTER: THE AMERICAN (1873–1889)

The ship *Hammonia* slowly pulled into New York Harbor through a cold sea breeze in the dawning light of March 27, 1873. It was a ship of the Hamburg America Line built by Caird & Company in 1866. The ship was a 3,035-gross-ton vessel, 340 feet in length, with a 40-foot beam of iron construction, two masts, one funnel (smokestack), a single screw (propeller) and a cruise speed of twelve knots.

The *Hammonia* made regular runs between Hamburg or Bremen, Germany, and New York City, as well as other ports of call on the eastern seaboard of the United States. The passage from Hamburg to New York City was about twelve days, depending on the weather in the North Atlantic. Passengers aboard were generally European emigrants streaming in from Germany, Austria, Russia, Poland and other countries to the United States and Canada between the years 1866 to 1878. The ship carried 678 passengers: 58 in first class, 120 in second class and 500 in third, the miserable confines and conditions of steerage.[14]

By midday, the *Hammonia* had docked. The passengers straggled to the immigrant-processing center at Castle Garden, the depot operated by the New York Board of Emigration Commissioners. They passed down the pier, where they were examined. If any health problems were noted, the immigrants were diverted to a hospital. They then entered the Garden and presented themselves at the desk located in the center of a very large room.

These passengers gave what information they could: their names and those of their families, the ship they were on, their point of destination, the route they wanted to take to reach their destination, the amount of money they brought with them and the number of pieces and weight of their luggage. Then they were shown to the baths.

There were large basins for bathing where a dozen or more people shared a space. Soap was plentiful. Every amenity then available was granted the newcomers so they could leave the facility clean.

There were no beds or overnight facilities, but a barge was available, without charge, for transport from Castle Garden to various train depots. The first step in a new land is always the hardest. The immigration personnel provided maps and did their best to give directions in the different languages. Sometimes it was enough to simply point the way.[15]

Among the immigrants arriving at Castle Garden that March morning was a young man traveling alone. He emerged from the squalid depths of steerage and lined up with the other five hundred passengers at the registration desk to provide the required information. The Castle Garden immigration record shows that the young man was Joseph Prinster and that he arrived on March 27, 1873, on the *Hammonia.* Other information included:

Point of departure: Hamburg & Harve, Germany
Age: 28
Occupation: laborer
Country of birth: Switzerland
Place of Birth: unknown
City or Village of Destination: United States
Price of ticket paid by: self

Left blank or designated "unknown" were his place of last residence, plan, passage, amount of money and names and addresses of relatives left behind. Equally blank were questions regarding whether he had been in the United

States before, whether he was going to meet someone in the country and, if so, what that relationship might be.[16]

Josef Pruenster had become Joseph Prinster, and he was a mystery. The date of his arrival is a clue to much more. If born in 1854, he was eighteen years old when he arrived in 1873, not twenty-eight, which also means that he must have avoided being drafted into the Austrian army.

Among the five hundred travelers in third-class passage were many fellow Austrians. Some had contacts in New York. They supported one another, practicing English, sharing plans and ideas for their destination, making contacts, finding temporary lodging and coming up with some means of supporting themselves.

At eighteen years of age, Joseph had rugged good looks and stood six feet, two inches tall. He had thick coal-black hair, deep searching brown eyes and often a thick brushy mustache. His hair was closely cropped, and his features were well proportioned. He had a friendly and inviting demeanor. There was an easy way about him, and he was courteous and kind. He carried himself in an almost military mien and walked with a sprightly and energetic stride.[17] He would have been a striking figure in any group or gathering.

With the help of friends from the ship, Joseph found some work and shelter while in New York. From his fellow workers and friends in the German/Austrian communities, he soon learned that other opportunities waited in the towns and new growing cities to the west.

He worked for a time in New York as a laborer until he learned of a promising new city on the Ohio River called Cincinnati. In the 1800s, Cincinnati was the largest pork-producing city in the world and one of the biggest cities in the American West. It had been given the nickname "Porkopolis." Beef and pork were processed and shipped down the Mississippi River to New Orleans and then redistributed.

Meatpacking was simple and primitive back then. The animals were slaughtered and the meat stuffed into brine-filled barrels for shipping. By the mid-nineteenth century, twenty-six different meat-processing plants operated there at full capacity. After the Civil War, pork operators and investors organized the Union Railroad Company Stockyard, a fifty-acre facility that could hold seventy-five thousand animals. Within three years, four other large processing companies had followed suit and built stockyards.

Cincinnati had a developed canal system leading to the Ohio and Mississippi Rivers. The city also had readily available salt deposits, which were essential to the industry. The manpower for these plants came from the influx of German immigrants working their way across America. A young Joseph Prinster made it to Cincinnati and started to work in the meat business.

The pork industry was profitable for the owners and provided steady work and decent pay for the workers, but it was not a pretty occupation. City residents built iron fences around their yards to keep out the hoards of pigs being driven to the stockyards and slaughterhouses. The canals ran red with blood and entrails, polluting the water. There was no need for trash collection. The swine roamed the sidewalks in the packinghouse district and consumed all the debris. There was no automation: this was all hands-on effort. The workers returned home at the end of the day covered in blood and animal waste.[18]

The work was cruel, but Joseph was ambitious and willing to work hard. He spent nearly ten years in the Cincinnati region doing this work and learning the butcher's trade. Eventually, he grew restless. He thought that there had to be more to America than working in this grueling industry. He read newspapers in order to improve his proficiency in reading and writing English. He heard of the western migration and a gold rush in the far West. As his English improved, he began to organize his plans for the next step in his future. With the help of friends in the German community, he applied to become a naturalized citizen of the United States of America.

On March 25, 1884, Joseph Prinster traveled to the probate court in Hillsboro, Ohio, the county seat of Highland County, a short distance from Cincinnati. There he made his "Declaration of Intention to become a Citizen of the United States of America." He declared under oath that it was his bona fide intention "to renounce forever all allegiance and fidelity to any Foreign Prince, Potentate, State or Sovereignty, and particularly to Francis Joseph Emperor of Austria whose subject he is." Not long afterward, Joseph headed west through Kansas and on to Colorado.[19]

Between the 1850s and the 1880s, a massive influx of German-speaking settlers found new homes in Kansas. Some came from their homelands in Europe, but most of them came from German communities in the eastern United States. They moved westward from Illinois, Pennsylvania, Indiana and Ohio. Many came because of the efforts of the Kansas Pacific and Santa Fe Railroads. These companies were in fierce competition to complete their rail lines across the state of Kansas during the 1870s, and to do so, they recruited immigrants, especially Germans, to Kansas.[20]

Part of the railroads' efforts was to sell their land grants and build up farms and communities adjacent to the railroads to manufacture products to haul as well as potential passengers. The German-speaking population in Kansas had become sizable by mid-1880.

But by 1884, Joseph Prinster was focused on gold in Colorado, not farming in Kansas. He traveled by train through the German colonies in Kansas and followed the gold rush to Cripple Creek, Colorado. His gold-mining efforts came to naught. He had to face failure as a gold miner and had to realize that a fortune in gold was not to be his.

The Santa Fe Railroad had completed a line to La Junta, Colorado, by 1876. It continued to extend the line over Raton Pass, then to Lamy (near Santa Fe) and westward to California. By 1884, La Junta had become a major depot for the Santa Fe Railroad, and there were plans to further expand shops and repair facilities. Joseph read about this in the newspapers and decided that La Junta might present employment opportunities.

Joseph arrived in La Junta in 1885. By 1886, he had obtained employment with Martin Stephens, a local businessman and a stockholder and director of the Bank of La Junta. Joseph also formed a partnership with a man named W.C. Koehler. The exact nature of these partnerships is unclear, but it is easy to assume from Joseph's activities that they were likely related to the cattle and meat business.

It was only a short time after arriving in La Junta that Joseph established himself in the business he knew best: meat processing. By 1888, he was running a successful operation with numerous livestock pens. Joseph made frequent trips to western Kansas to purchase carloads of sheep and cattle for his slaughterhouse. Often in the fall, he would make several such trips per month, at times purchasing three carloads of corn-fed beef. The operations also generated a vigorous business in animal hides, processing pork and lambs and smoking and curing meats.[21]

Before long, Joseph had expanded into the retail meat business. On December 29, 1887, he placed an announcement in the *La Junta Tribune* reading, "J.F. Prinster will open a Meat Market about January 1st in the building occupied by the Strauss Brothers in Trinidad Plaza."

The Palace Meat Market indeed opened in January 1888 and offered for sale "beef, pork, mutton, veal, poultry & fish." This retail venture was a partnership with Mr. W.C. Koehler. The two men operated the business for several years and gradually made improvements to the facility. In April 1889, the *Tribune* reported, "Prinster and Koehler received a large marble slab," apparently for the countertop in their market. In modern-day terms, Joseph was now "vertically integrated" and apparently doing well, yet the partnership with Koehler ended in June of that same year. Joseph published a notice of the "Dissolution of the Partnership" in the *La Junta Tribune* stating that W.C. Koehler was retiring and Prinster was assuming all the debts.[22]

Joseph was now well known among the stockmen of the area and the businessmen of the community. The partnership dissolution with Koehler, however, was not the only change in Joseph's life in 1889. He was now approaching thirty-five years of age. His efforts in the meat-processing business were paying off. During his travels, especially those to Wichita, Kansas, he had become acquainted with the German communities.

It was in Sedgwick County, Kansas, that he met a young woman who had recently arrived from Moravia, a country that was part of the Austro-Hungarian empire. She was only nineteen, tall, attractive and very intelligent. She spoke his native German and was diligently studying English. She had arrived with her younger brother, Joseph, and was living with her sister, Mary, and working as a domestic maid in Wichita. Her name was Bohemilla Kroboth, and she was called Millie.[23]

Backstory Notes

I have searched for ten years to find the precise date and place that Joseph Prinster entered the United States. The search included the help of genealogy experts, examination of immigration and naturalization records, shipping lists, immigration port records, passport applications, census records, family letters and records and memories of Joseph's descendants.

A search on Ancestry.com of the New York passenger lists, 1829–1957, lists "Jos Pranster" arriving in New York on February 1883. His place of origin is given as Austria, and he departed Bremen, Germany, sailing on the *Donau* and arriving in the port of New York, United States of America. His estimated birth date is 1855, and he is twenty-eight. Joseph Prinster was born in 1854 and would have been twenty-nine in November 1883. I do not believe, however, that "Jos Pranster" on the ship *Donau* is the Joseph Prinster of Riffian, South Tyrol. The Castle Garden immigration list is the one used as the basis of the information for this book. That list names a passenger, Joseph Prinster, occupation laborer, age twenty-eight, arriving at the port of New York on March 27, 1873, on the ship *Hammonia*. It gives his birth country and country of origin as Switzerland. All other information about this Joseph Prinster is either unknown or simply left blank, including the amount of money he carried, which was always carefully tracked and recorded by the Castle Garden officials.

The other sources relied on are the passport applications filed by Joseph's sons, Frank and Leo, in May 1920. The applications were accompanied by an affidavit signed by Joseph, so presumably Joseph was aware of the information given. The application notes that their father, Joseph, entered the United States from Bremen, Germany, on or about March 24, 1876, presumably information provided by their father. The assumption is made in this book that the Castle Garden immigration record information is most likely Joseph Prinster of Riffian, South Tyrol, and La Junta, Colorado. The time sequence for the 1883 entry of "Jos Pranster" on the New York passenger list does not work because of ample information that shows that Joseph worked in the United States ten or more years before arriving in La Junta in 1885 or 1886. It is entirely possible that for the passport application, Joseph did not accurately remember the year of his entry. He is off by three years, but the month is correct. In 1873, the year the *Hammonia* landed at Castle Garden, Joseph would have been eighteen years and three months old.

He was a tall man and had a dark mustache, perhaps a beard, and might well have passed for twenty-eight years old, as the record notes. The Castle Garden record states twice that Joseph Prinster's place of origin was Switzerland. We know now that that is not the case, but Joseph, or someone on his behalf, gave that same information to the census bureau for its 1910 survey.

The border of Switzerland is a very short distance from Riffian. Today, you can drive to Switzerland for lunch and be back in time for afternoon coffee. If Joseph had arrived in 1873, this would have allowed time for Joseph to spend ten years working in the United States before arriving in La Junta in 1885 or 1886. We also know by his intent to become a citizen that he was in Cincinnati, Ohio, in 1884. There are numerous family records and correspondence that "he left home when he was very young." This seems to suggest that he left South Tyrol before his nineteenth birthday, the age he would have been required to enter the military. Instead, he headed to Switzerland, a neutral country, and then found his way onto a ship headed for America, probably in 1873, when he was eighteen years old.

BOHEMILLA "MILLIE" KROBOTH PRINSTER (1870–1939)

She must have turned heads, this stately seventeen-year-old beauty stepping off the ship *North German Lloyd* in Baltimore, Maryland, in 1887, holding the hand of her twelve-year-old brother, Joseph. There were no family members there to greet them, and she spoke little English. She faced a challenge: find her way to Wichita, Kansas, where her two older sisters lived. Was she fearful? One can only speculate. If so, Bohemilla Kroboth would not be one to show it.

It is easy to imagine her searching for someone who spoke German or Czech to help her find the train station. There were many Germans living in Maryland. She would be careful with what little money she had, perhaps spending it on food for Joseph while going hungry herself. She was a "good Catholic girl." She would ignore the stares of men, young and old, who certainly must have ogled her. They may have wondered if she was married, if Joseph was her son and why someone so young and pretty was traveling without an escort.

What did she think of the landscape that flashed past the train window? It was 1,200 miles from Baltimore to Wichita, and once past the green Appalachian Mountains, it was flat, brown and boring. She might have wondered if "wild Indians" still stalked the rough frontier towns she saw as the train rumbled on. The haphazard architecture was a stark contrast to the charming villages, surrounded by lush green hills and dark forests, of her homeland in Hohenstadt, Moravia, Austria. It had been a long and arduous trip so far, but the boring landscape was not important. She longed to be reunited with her sisters; the drab views were negligible.

Her sister Marie Anna was nineteen when she left Austria seven years earlier, accompanied by their sister Josephine (age unknown). The sisters had first settled in Tell City, Indiana. The two worked in a hotel and saved their money in the hope of returning home to their mother in Hohenstadt, but their mother died soon after they arrived. They remained in Indiana, where they became acquainted with the Simon family.

In 1883, Marie Anna (or "Mary") married Joseph Peter Simon, the oldest son of John Stephen Simon, who had emigrated from Prussia in 1850. This Joseph was probably a farmer like his father, as were most of the Simon family members who now lived in Kansas. Joseph and Mary eventually would have seven children. Their two oldest boys, William and Nicholas, were toddlers when Millie arrived at their home in the spring of 1887.[24]

As Millie's train rolled past the flat plains and wheat fields of Kansas, she probably thought about her two older siblings, Bohuslav and Claudine, who had stayed behind in Hohenstadt. She no doubt reflected on her beloved mother, Josepha, now deceased, who had held the family together while

Joseph Prinster stood tall, had a sprightly gait and "was always good to poor people," according to Millie. *Courtesy of Miriam Peckham.*

Joseph and Millie on their wedding day, October 19, 1889. *Courtesy of Miriam Peckham.*

their father, Dominic, traveled extensively collecting taxes for the Austrian government. Millie hoped that someday their family would be reunited.

Once they arrived in Wichita, Millie (and probably little Joseph as well) lived with Mary and Joseph Simon. Millie was soon earning money as a domestic, learning English and participating in the various activities of her close-knit German community.

Within a year, she caught the eye of a tall, handsome fellow Austrian named Joseph Prinster, sixteen years her senior. Joseph would have been mature enough to not be intimidated by this striking young woman's strong personality and industrious ways. He was, in fact, drawn to them. And how could she not resist him? He was not only tall and good-looking, but he had also already established himself in business in a little town in Colorado called La Junta.

Millie and Joseph's wedding, held on October 18, 1889, was performed by Reverend John Lacouvich, a Catholic priest, in a small town near Wichita in Sedgwick County, Kansas. An approving family and numerous well-wishers surrounded them. Joseph would be thirty-five in November, and Millie had turned nineteen a few months before.[25] They now were traveling to La Junta, where they would make their home and build their future for the next forty years.

LA JUNTA, COLORADO: QUEEN CITY OF THE ARKANSAS VALLEY (1889–1900)

As the Santa Fe train headed west from Wichita, Joseph must have reflected proudly on his life thus far as he gazed at his beautiful young wife. Millie would fill a void and make his life complete.

He had known her about a year and had observed how hardworking and intelligent she was. She had a natural ability for languages and had already become fluent in reading and speaking English. She had told him about her early school days in Moravia, where she had learned the Czech language as well as her native German. She also was very capable in math, was outspoken with ideas of her own and was strong-willed—as he soon learned. For Joseph, Millie had all the qualifications for a capable and excellent helpmate.

When they first met, Millie asked many questions about this strange-sounding place, La Junta, pronounced "la hoonta." He told her that La Junta was Spanish for "the junction." Before she would consider marrying him and settling there, she wanted to be sure that there were schools, churches and medical facilities. After they had become engaged to be married, Joseph took her on several visits to La Junta. On the last of these trips, she and Joseph looked for a place to start a home. They found a tract of ground and a small house that appealed to Millie. It also suited Joseph's pocketbook, so he put down a deposit on the property.

It was a tract of three lots at the intersection of Belleview Avenue and Fourth Street at the northeast corner of Block 46 of the town of La Junta. Belleview Avenue runs southward out of the center of town, and it served a residential area on a hill overlooking the town, the train depot and the Arkansas River to the north. One month after their marriage, Joseph purchased two of three adjoining lots for $225, and on December 16, 1889, he purchased the third lot and a house for $525. The newlyweds now had their home. Three years later, in 1892, Joseph obtained a mortgage on these lots from the Otero County Building and Loan and transferred full ownership of them to Millie.[26]

In order to insulate the family home from any future claims from creditors and to ensure that his bride would always have a home in the event that something happened to him, Joseph, and then later his sons, would follow the practice of making sure that their wives owned the houses they lived in.

La Junta was now a very different place than the small railroad town Joseph had discovered five years earlier on his way to Cripple Creek. The town had been incorporated in 1881, and in those early years, it served as a stopping place for the Santa Fe Railroad. Some cattle and sheep were raised in the surrounding area, and farming existed on a small scale, enough to fulfill local needs but not exportation. Beginning in the 1880s, a large influx of settlers came from Kansas and other states, encouraged in part by the efforts of the Santa Fe Railroad. The Santa Fe sold its land grant real estate to prospective farmers, thereby increasing the population and the production of livestock and crops to be transported to eastern markets by the railroad.

When the Santa Fe rail line was first completed to Pueblo in 1876, La Junta was just a temporary stopping place for the Atchison, Topeka and Santa Fe Railroad. At this time, La Junta had a population of about five hundred people. As the line completed its extension southward to Trinidad and across Raton Pass to New Mexico, the little town of La Junta grew. The railroad company recognized the future of the La Junta station and built a fine depot, roundhouses and repair shops. It made La Junta the headquarters of its Colorado division. This expansion in the mid-1880s is what had caught Joseph's attention and encouraged his move from Cripple Creek to La Junta in 1885.

The growth in La Junta was rapid, and by 1890, Joseph and his business acquaintances loved to brag that the population had grown to 2,500 and that, in addition, there were forty-thousand acres of grazing land, eighteen thousand head of cattle, 7,500 sheep, 4,800 horses and 366 mules. La Junta was becoming a strong commercial center. Houses were being built and occupied. The town boasted four churches: Baptist, Catholic, Episcopal and Methodist. It had three newspapers: the *Tribune*, the *Otero County Democrat* and the *La Junta Watermelon*. It also had an opera house, a fine hospital and an elegant schoolhouse that had cost $12,000.[27] A rapidly growing western town like La Junta offered many opportunities, and Millie would have recognized this and been impressed by it.

As the newlyweds made their way across the plains of eastern Colorado, Millie and Joseph discussed their plans for the future. Joseph probably reminisced briefly about his childhood in South Tyrol and his journey from there to the Cincinnati packinghouses and then to La Junta. He was thankful for his turn of good fortune and now for Millie. He might have thought fleetingly about the Alps. He hoped that someday he would see them again, but that would have to wait. Right now, his life was on these flat, brown and vast plains.

Joseph owned and operated a small store in La Junta, Colorado. *Author's collection.*

Joseph was a hard worker and always a risk-taker. He had already made a name for himself in La Junta, so when he and Millie arrived there, they were greeted by some fanfare and an article in the *La Junta Tribune* describing the details of their wedding: "J.F. Prinster surprised some of his friends by returning from Kansas last Sunday night with a bride. Everyone supposed that 'Joe' had gone east to purchase another car load of fat cows, but it seems that his mind was on another more important matter. The bride was Miss Amelia [*sic*] Kroboth of Wichita, Kansas, and the ceremony performed at that place last Saturday."[28]

Joseph's Colorado Meat Packing Company and Palace Meat Market were established and operating, processing cattle and sheep and smoking and curing meats. Joseph made sausages from recipes he had learned in South Tyrol and improved on during his Cincinnati years. Now he also set a goal to settle and raise a family by being careful with his money.

The agriculture industry was in full swing in Otero County, and acquiring raw acreage to develop into productive farmland seemed a good business venture. In 1820, Congress adopted legislation that made possible the sale of public lands for the statutory price of $1.25 per acre. Joseph made plans to take advantage of this opportunity.

On November 25, 1889, one month after his marriage, Joseph made a claim at the Federal Land Office in Pueblo for 160 acres of land. He paid $1.25 per acre, a total of $200.00. This was the beginning of a lifelong project for Joseph. In later years, his grandchildren referred to it as a "sorry piece of land." He obtained multiple mortgages and expended considerable effort to develop it. The land not only needed to be improved and developed, but in Joseph's view, more land also had to be acquired.

Joseph's passion for owning real estate was understandable. Being a landowner in Austria was an almost impossible dream. In America, he could buy all the land he could afford, and he set about doing just that.

The land required water, so Joseph immediately set to work to build a ditch and buy water rights. With money borrowed from friends and acquaintances and from the Farm Land Mortgage Company, he proceeded with his venture. The ditch was designated "the Prinster Ditch" and was built to carry 1.44 cfs (cubic feet of water per second), the rights for which Joseph acquired from the Otero Canal Company in 1892 for a cost of $800. In July 1894, Joseph purchased more property, this time 120 acres in Section 10 of the same township and range. The Prinster Ditch delivered water to parts of this tract also. It is not known today what the land produced or how it was used. Joseph received a deed to this land from the United States of

America in 1896 and owned the land throughout his life, using it as leverage to purchase more land.[29]

As Joseph's meatpacking and processing businesses grew and his real estate transactions continued, Joseph and Millie started their family. Their first son, Paul Henry, was born on July 6, 1890, and the *La Junta Tribune* made note of the event in its July 12 edition.

Joseph had many ideas and the energy to carry them out, but perhaps more importantly, he always seemed to have the ability to innovate and adapt his business to the demands of the times. Economic conditions were becoming difficult in the 1890s, and La Junta was beginning to suffer the impact. In late 1889, the Palace Meat Market was having difficulty collecting its accounts receivable. To deal with that problem, Joseph ran the following ad in the *La Junta Tribune*: "Palace Meat Market. J.F. Prinster. After October Pay Day I will sell for CASH ONLY."

A year and a half later, a similar problem arose in the slaughter and processing business. In October 1891, Joseph published the following:

> *NOTICE: After the first of November a change will take place and my business will be known as the La Junta Packing Company and I will sell for CASH ONLY. Prices will be put away* [sic] *down making it an object for the people to pay cash and save money. All who are indebted to me will please settle before the 5th of November as I will place my books in the hands of a collector. Thanking you for your patronage and hoping to receive a share of it in the future.*
>
> *I remain Yours Truly, J.F. Prinster.*

Joseph was in business when the financial panic of 1893 hit the country hard, particularly in Colorado. Banks throughout the country failed, as did the Northern Pacific, the Union Pacific and the Santa Fe Railroads. The Santa Fe Railroad went into receivership in December 1893.

Some accounts suggest that Joseph may have been forced to close his store during this time and that he traveled to Bisbee, Arizona, to work in the copper mines, leaving Millie at home caring for their two small sons. Paul was now three, and Frank (born on November 10, 1892) was a year old.

But by 1894, Joseph was negotiating new business deals and expanding his family. (Leo was born in 1895, Andrew in 1896 and Mary in 1899.) That same year, 1894, Joseph—in partnership with James McNeen, an implement and equipment dealer in La Junta, and C.W. Baumgardner, a lumber dealer and builder—borrowed $1,000 from the Otero County Building and Loan and assumed an additional $200 second mortgage to purchase two lots in downtown La Junta between Third and Fourth Streets on Cimarron Avenue. Joseph also borrowed $750 for equipment. The venture became Prinster's Market and Butcher Shop. There was now a retail outlet for the Colorado Meat Packing Company products and a venue for selling other products.

In 1902, the sixth child and fifth son, Edward, was born on May 3. Their family continued to grow, and Joseph and Millie continued to acquire more real estate. An acquaintance of Joseph's by the name of J.P. Bradish had platted some land called the Bradish Addition. There was already a Bradish Avenue on the east boundary of the city, and now additional lots were platted in the new addition at the north end of Bradish Avenue on the north side of the town between the Santa Fe Railroad and the Arkansas River.

In May 1902, Joseph bought four lots in the Bradish subdivision, and three years later, he purchased an additional four lots across the street. This location served as the family's new home until the early 1920s.[30] This was the home in which the other three children were born and raised. After Edward, Clarence was born in December 1904, followed by the second daughter,

Left to right: Mary, Joseph, Paul, Andrew, Millie, Edward, Frank and Leo Prinster, 1902. *Author's collection, received from Tayana Pruenster in 1995.*

Outdoor sports were Lucille Prinster's greatest joy, especially basketball. *Courtesy of Miriam Peckham.*

Lucille, on June 17, 1907. Their last child, Joseph, was born on October 10, 1909, when Millie was thirty-nine years old.

From 1900 to 1939, many daunting events occurred in the Prinster family—some good, some devastating and some tragic. Together, Joseph and Millie faced each challenge with fortitude, determination and an amazing resilience.

Backstory Notes

The fate of Joseph and the Palace Meat Market is not known for certain. An article in the *Grand Junction Daily Sentinel* in 1950, at the time of the opening of the City Market at Ninth Street and North Avenue, gave the following account of Joseph Prinster: "He settled in La Junta where he would get into his own business of meat selling. He bought a modest little place in 1885 and ran it successfully as one of the city's pioneer merchants until 1893. That was the panic year and the Prinster shop went to the wall with many of its fellow retail places. Mr. Prinster went back to mining, this time in Bisbee,

Arizona. But in 1900 he came back to La Junta with a stake big enough to again go into business there."

This is the only reference found to Joseph closing his business or going to Bisbee to work in the copper mines and not returning until 1900. The *Daily Sentinel* writer did not attribute the quote to any person or source. Between December 1893 and July 1894, the *La Junta Tribune* contained ads for the Palace Market, and for the years up until 1898, real estate records indicate that Joseph was actively involved in real estate transactions and retail business locations in downtown La Junta. On April 16, 1898, the *La Junta Tribune* reported that J.F. Prinster would open a first-class meat market in a location previously occupied by the Palace Restaurant and would sell porterhouse steaks for fifteen cents and pork chops for eight cents per pound.

Interviews with the grandchildren of Joseph Prinster do not reveal any knowledge of stories or accounts from their parents or others of Joseph going to Bisbee to work in the mines. His granddaughter Miriam (Blevins) Peckham stated that she believes Joseph remained in La Junta and did not travel to work in Bisbee, Arizona.

TRIALS AND TRIUMPHS OF JOSEPH AND MILLIE (1900–1939)

In 1900, Millie and Joseph celebrated their eleventh wedding anniversary. In this short span of time, they had seen many of their dreams fulfilled and had endured a few setbacks. Always working as a team, they were involved in numerous real estate transactions and would continue to invest in more. As soon as they paid off one, they invested in another, borrowing from banks, loan companies and private individuals. Joseph proudly paid off their federal land grant patent in 1896 and then remortgaged it several times in order to buy more real estate.

They had survived the financial panic of 1893 and the Santa Fe Railroad's receivership that same year. In 1898, their barn and outbuildings burned to the ground while they were away, and two years later, Joseph survived a serious illness that was noted in the *Tribune*.

They now had six children, ages one to ten years old. The town of La Junta was growing and prospering, and despite a few bumps in the road, so was the Prinster family. Millie's nephew, Bohuslav Jr., came to live with them in 1900. Young Bohuslav had been eight years old in 1892 when his parents immigrated to America with him and his cousin, John. Bohuslav's mother had died, and his father sent the sixteen-year-old to live briefly with his sister Millie's family. Young Bohuslav would have been a welcomed addition to the Prinster family.

Like his Aunt Millie, he was a devout Roman Catholic. At age twenty-two, he went into the seminary at the University of Austria in Innsbruck, just over the mountain from Joseph's family home in Riffian. While in the seminary, he met Father Edward Joseph Flanagan, the founder of Boys Town, and they became lifelong friends. Upon completion of his studies, Millie's nephew changed his name from Bohuslav to Timothy (the name means "honoring God") and returned to the United States in 1911.[31] He remained close to Millie and her family for the rest of his life. Interestingly, Edward Prinster, who was born in 1902 during Bohuslav's stay with the family, followed his cousin into the priesthood twenty-two years later.

By 1900, the Prinster Market had become a retail outlet for Joseph's meatpacking plant, and the family was prominent enough for the newspapers to take notice of significant events in their lives, both personal and relating to the business. Between 1900 and 1902, several such items appeared in the *La Junta Tribune*. Joseph's typhoid fever is mentioned, a lawsuit by the City of La Junta against Joseph Prinster in 1901 was noted and an accident involving one of the Prinster children made news in 1902.

The 1901 lawsuit revealed another side to Joseph's personality. Always remembered as kind and soft-spoken, Joseph became enraged when the city slapped a five-dollar fine on him for "violating the ordinance regulating the use of water." Joseph hired an attorney and took the case to court. A jury found him guilty, and in addition to the five dollars, he was ordered to pay court costs.

"Mr. Prinster will have to pay $75 for the privilege of watering his lawn outside the hours prescribed," trumpeted the newspaper. Two months later, Joseph was hauled into court again and fined ten dollars for rendering lard in the back of his market.

On Wednesday, May 14, 1902, the *La Junta Tribune* reported, "The five-year-old son of J.F. Prinster [Andrew] was badly injured Saturday morning while playing about the butcher shop. He knocked a cleaver from one of the blocks and was struck in the leg making a very ugly wound, five stitches being required to close it."[32]

Sometime during this same period, Millie's younger brother, Joseph, who had come to America with her in 1887, had opened a meat market in Swink,

Millie's younger brother, Joe Kroboth, in his store in Swink, Colorado. *Author's collection.*

a small town five miles from La Junta. He would have been about twenty-two years old, and it is assumed that he also had been living with the Prinsters while working for Joseph and learning the meat market trade. According to *F.A. McKinney's Otero and Crowley County Directory*, by 1914 Joe Kroboth was operating a meat market in Swink (most likely with Joe Prinster's financing and help).

Millie had her hands full, raising children and running a household with extra mouths to feed and laundry to do. She most decidedly was the disciplinarian in the family. Her grandchildren remembered her years later as strict and "scary." Millie ran an organized and efficient home and continued to be involved in the family's real estate transactions.

In about 1904, a crisis affected the family's finances, enough so that Joseph pulled his sons Paul, age thirteen, and Frank, age eleven, out of school to work full time for him in his market. How the boys felt about this is not known, but Paul, who was often truant from school, was probably relieved. It upset Millie terribly, however. Education was important to her, and she and Joseph presumably locked horns over it. Obviously Joseph prevailed,

Millie, Lucille and niece Millie Simon on their way to visit relatives in Swink. *Courtesy of Dan Prinster and the Joseph C. Prinster family.*

and these young boys, out of necessity, went into training as meat cutters and butchers.[33]

Four years after the boys went to work for their father, their meat market was burglarized twice in the same month. The May 30, 1908 edition of the *La Junta Tribune* reported that "Joe Prinster's meat market was burglarized for the second time within a month. As in the first instance, an entrance was effected through the rear door and the cash register was relieved of between $4 and $5 in change. The burglar overlooked a bet in not tackling the safe, which contained a considerable sum of money. Although the safe door was closed, it was not locked, and Joe is not feeling as much aggrieved over his loss as he might have been had the cracksman had his eyes open—already yet [*sic*]."[34]

By 1910, the family was living in a larger home on five lots in the Bradish Addition. The La Junta City Directory shows Joseph Prinster, head of household; Millie, wife; Paul, nineteen; Frank, seventeen; Leo, fifteen; Andrew, fourteen; Mary, ten; Edward, seven; Clarence, five; Lucille, three; and baby Joseph, six months. Three months later, in August 1910, little Joseph died. He would be the first of the nine Prinster children to die.

In 1909, Joseph received word that his mother, Maria Gruener, had died. On December 28, 1909, Joseph asked Millie to write a letter in reply to his family. He instructed them to use his share of the inheritance to have ten masses said for his parents and his siblings. Any remaining money was to be given to his younger brother, Antonius. He proudly announced to them that he had a new son. His name was Joseph, and he was two and a half months old.

"Thank God," he wrote, "we are all healthy and we hope the same for you." Joseph had also apparently been told that his younger sister, Anna, was going to travel to America. "Dear sister," he wrote, "we are pleased to hear that you're getting ready to come over here. I will give you 20 dollars per month. The salary is from 12 dollars upward. I wonder whether Anton would like to come? I'd have work for him too—I'll give him 25 dollars and his food—that is when he comes alone? Does he bring his family or does he come alone?"

He then offered his sister some advice on travel and observations on conditions in America:

> *Dear sister, you must be supplied with warm clothes because it is very cold on the water. I hope you will soon get ready and come…weather was very cold here the last 4 weeks we have an early winter this year. The times are*

not so good in America the last 4 years have deteriorated. But that has not to do with us much—so I and the family greets you warmly—and hope to see you soon.

With best, best wishes for the new year, I remain your dear brother Joseph.

Joseph must have been longing to see his family and was willing to help them however he could. Neither his younger sister nor his brother Antonius made the journey.[35]

In 1912, Joseph and Millie's oldest son, Paul, age twenty-two, married Carrie Palmer—a marriage that ended tragically four years later with Carrie's death. Their two-year-old son, Paul Joseph (also known as Paul Jr.), was then taken in and raised by Millie. That same year, Millie and Joseph's

Leo had worked in the railroad yards for less than a year when he suffered the accident that cost him his leg. *Courtesy of Dan Prinster and the Joseph C. Prinster family.*

son Andrew, age sixteen, died of a mastoid infection of the bones around the ear.

Two years later, their nineteen-year-old son Leo left the family business to work for the Santa Fe Railroad in La Junta, a decision that was to cost him dearly. Leo had been working for less than a year when his foot got caught in a switch and was crushed. Gangrene set in, and two years and three operations later, his leg was amputated below the knee.

An attractive young nurse who had recently arrived in La Junta from Illinois, Freda Wilson, tended him during his recovery. They fell in love and married two years after his accident. Leo returned to work in the family business as a meat cutter.

In May 1916, Joseph opened another meat market in Lamar, Colorado, an event noted by the *La Junta Tribune*: "John Schmeider, who has been employed as a meat cutter at Prinster's for the past three years, left the first of the week for Lamar where he will have charge of a meat market which Mr. Prinster has recently opened in that city."[36]

Grandma Jody and son Frank Jr. enjoying a nice afternoon in the park, circa 1916. *Courtesy of Dan Prinster and the Joseph C. Prinster family.*

The Prinsters' three oldest sons were now married. Frank married Josephine Patterson on June 22, 1914. Widower Paul married again in April 1919; his second wife was Edna Lampson. These marriages added four grandchildren to the lives of Joseph and Millie. Frank and Josephine had two children: Frank Jr., born in 1915, and Josephine, born in 1917. Paul had his oldest son, Paul Jr., and a daughter, Billie Mae, with Edna. Leo and Freda had no children.

Joseph and Millie's younger children—Mary (twenty-one), Edward (nineteen), Clarence (seventeen) and Lucille (fifteen)—still lived at the family home on Bradish Avenue. By 1920, all of their children were working in the family meat market and grocery business, but they were no longer working for Joseph. Paul and Frank had bought Joseph out, and their siblings now worked for them, allowing Joseph to retire.

In addition to owning a large tract of land in the Bradish Addition, which was now the family compound, Joseph and Millie accumulated numerous parcels of land throughout the town of La Junta between 1914 and 1920. According to Millie's edict, when the sons were married and starting their own families, they were expected to rent one of these properties from her if they moved away from the Bradish complex. It was well known and passed down to grandchildren that the wives did not like this arrangement. After

The family gathered together to celebrate Joseph and Millie's twenty-fifth wedding anniversary. *Courtesy of Miriam Peckham.*

Paul married his second wife, Edna, and Leo received his settlement from the railroad, both couples bought lots in their own names. It is not known if the two sons bought these lots from Joseph and Millie. Frank and Jody remained Millie's tenants until they left La Junta in 1924. Millie's efforts to control her sons and their families were nothing short of relentless.[37]

The early years of the Roaring Twenties were golden, particularly for Millie. She and Joseph had time to travel. They were financially secure and owned considerable property in La Junta, including a hotel near the railroad depot and numerous rental properties. While most of the nation was jumping onto the prosperous gravy train of Wall Street investments, Millie and Joseph put their money into more real estate. Millie bought her dream home in downtown La Junta at 401 Raton. It was a magnificent, stately, two-story, white colonial-style house. The purchase price was $15,000, a princely sum in those days.

Millie's home was a magnificent, stately, two-story, white colonial-style house purchased for the princely sum of $15,000. *Back, left to right*: Frank, Leo, Jody, Edward, Freda and Clarence. *Middle, left to right*: Mary, Millie, Joseph, Lucille and Paul. *Bottom, left to right*: Paul Jr., Josephine and Frank Jr. Image circa 1922. *Courtesy of Miriam Peckham.*

They also purchased three more lots on Colorado Avenue, the same street where their sons' meat market and Millie's hotel were located. By 1922, they had also bought six more lots in the Bradish area for $300.[38]

Not being one to take a backseat in her life, Millie decided that she would learn to drive. She purchased a used Hupmobile and taught herself to drive forward—but not backward. Whenever she needed to back up, she turned off the engine, trekked to the family meat market and imposed on one of her sons to come to her rescue. She caused quite a sensation in town because she was the first woman in La Junta to drive a car.[39]

The Hupmobile was created in 1909 by Robert Craig Hupp. It had an original sticker price of $750, which included a seventeen-horsepower four-cylinder engine and sliding gear transmission.

Millie apparently dominated her three daughters-in-law. Sundays were the husbands' only day off, and the wives wanted to have some private time with them, but Millie would have none of it. She made it mandatory that everyone in the family attend Sunday dinner at her beautiful new home, every week. Her sons were not willing to defy her, so they all went.

Josephine and Frank's son, Teo, remembered his mother's feelings about those Sunday dinners: "I know that one of the things that was required of the married boys who lived there [La Junta] was to go over to Grandma and Grandpa's house every Sunday for dinner. My mother did not like that at all.

Automobiles were all the rage, and Millie decided that she, too, would learn to drive. She purchased a used Hupmobile and was the first woman in La Junta to drive an automobile. *Courtesy of Dan Prinster and the Joseph C. Prinster family.*

The Prinsters gathered for dinner at 401 Raton at Millie's insistence. *Courtesy of Miriam Peckham.*

She had her own family there [in town]. The men smoked cigars and drank whiskey, and the women did all the work."[40]

In 1920, Millie enraged Frank's and Leo's wives when she insisted that her two sons travel to Europe to check out a notice of an inheritance she had received from a long-lost relative. The supposed bequest proved to be a hoax, and when Frank and Leo returned home, their wives weren't speaking to them.

Between 1920 and 1924, numerous events took place in the Prinster family that would change their lives and would set Paul, Frank and Leo on a course that would define their destiny.

By 1920, Paul and Frank had sold Prinster Market, and in 1921, they opened City Market and Grocery Store at 116 Second Street. Around then, Leo had received a settlement from the railroad for his accident, and he used his money to invest in real estate. Also in 1920, he invested in a downtown business lot with his father in the 100 block of Colorado Avenue. Two years later, he and Freda bought an entire business block at First Street and Santa

Millie was an imposing but generous woman. The quintessential pioneer, she bore, raised and educated nine children; managed her real estate investments; and maintained discipline and stability in the family. *Courtesy of Dan Prinster and the Joseph C. Prinster family.*

Above: Paul, Frank and Leo were a "bond" of brothers in all their endeavors. *Courtesy of Miriam Peckham.*

Right: Jody, Clarence, twins Marjorie and Mary, Josephine and Annie Kroboth in La Junta, circa 1923. *Courtesy of Dan Prinster and the Joseph C. Prinster family.*

Fe Avenue from the La Junta Hardware Store, which Leo turned into a pool hall and barbershop. Joseph continued to accumulate lots in the Bradish Addition, as well as other locations in downtown La Junta. In July 1923, after three years of operation, Frank and Paul sold City Market and Grocery Store to businessmen from Rocky Ford. In March of the following year, Leo sold his pool hall on Santa Fe.[41]

Despite the Prinster family's prosperity, the year 1923 also brought heartache. In the spring of 1923, Millie became seriously ill and was sent to a Denver hospital for treatment. While she was recovering, her sixteen-year-old daughter Lucille suffered a serious mastoid infection, the same illness that had taken her brother Andrew's life eleven years earlier. Lucille was taken to the same Denver hospital where Millie had recently been treated. Lucille died on June 8, 1923, two days following an operation. Her obituary in the *La Junta Tribune* described an outstanding young woman:

> *Lucille Prinster was born in La Junta on June 15, 1907, and died just seven days before her sixteenth birthday. For two years she had been a student at Loretto Academy in Pueblo; the past two years she had spent at home and attended the high school, this year being a sophomore. Her literary talent was known to all her student friends, and her ability to write poetry was marked. A tribute recently written by her to a school friend was of such high order that it was highly praised and commented on by her instructors. She was a leader in all class activities, and was treasurer of her class. Out-of-door sports were her delight and none took a greater interest in basketball. She was a faithful member of the Catholic Church, being a member of the Young Ladies' Sodality and a teacher in the junior department of the Sunday school.*[42]

The entire community extended their sympathy to the bereaved parents for the loss of one so young and with such promise and hope for the future. Four days after her funeral, Frank and Josephine welcomed their twins, Marjorie and Mary, into the world, joining their siblings Frank Jr., now eight, and Josephine, who was six.

Sometime before 1924, Paul and Edna divorced after four years of marriage, and Paul was ready for a new start. In the fall of that year, he bought a snappy red Buick roadster and headed to Grand Junction. His father had spoken highly of Grand Junction as a good place to start a business after visiting there several years earlier.

Lucille died from a mastoid infection at the young age of sixteen. *Courtesy of Miriam Peckham.*

In June 1924, Joseph and Millie's daughter Mary married Donald Blevins, who had been courting her for five years. It was a major social event in La Junta, with a lengthy write-up in the *Daily Democrat*, which noted on August

Left: Jody was often seen with her children and neighbor children. *Courtesy of Dan Prinster and the Joseph C. Prinster family.*

Below: Jody with twins Marjorie and Mary. *Courtesy of Dan Prinster and the Joseph C. Prinster family.*

11 that "Miss Mary Prinster and Donald Blevins were united in marriage at 9 o'clock this morning in St. Patrick's church, with solemn high mass and with all the solemnity of the Catholic Church."[43]

It was a stylish wedding, with violins accompanying several soloists. Mary's gown and those of her bridesmaids were described in detail, along with the elegant décor of the church. Joseph and Millie hosted an elaborate breakfast at their Raton Street mansion, and Mary and Donald left for their honeymoon by train for a tour of Canada that included a cruise up the St. Lawrence River to Quebec.

The year 1924 also marked a period of change for Joseph and Millie. By that autumn, Leo and Frank had also moved to Grand Junction with their families and teamed up with Paul in the grocery business. The following year marked another milestone in Joseph's life. On June 9, 1925, he was issued a Certificate of Naturalization. At the age of seventy-one, Joseph Frank Prinster became a citizen of the United States.

In the meantime, Mary and Donald now lived in Denver, and Joseph and Millie's son Edward had entered college at the University of Notre

Joseph and Millie hosted an elaborate reception for daughter Mary and Donald Blevins at their Raton Street home on their wedding day. *Courtesy of Miriam Peckham.*

Joseph was a determined pioneer, a devoted father, a businessman and a civic leader. "His years exceeded the allotted span of three score and ten." *Author's collection.*

Dame in Indiana. In 1929, he entered the seminary in Denver to study for the priesthood. That left only Clarence at home. When Clarence turned twenty-two in 1926, he also left La Junta to join his brothers. Millie's big home was now a lonely, empty place. No more family gatherings and the

Joseph and Millie were devoted to each other and spent much of their time together in their golden years. *Courtesy of Dan Prinster and the Joseph C. Prinster family.*

laughter of grandchildren. No more holiday and birthday celebrations or family dinners. She sold the Raton Street house in 1927, and she and Joseph moved into one of their apartments.

One month after the stock market crash in October 1929, Millie's beloved Joseph died at age seventy-five. Millie wrote the sad news to Antonius, Joseph's brother, in a letter dated April 10, 1930:

> *My dear relatives;*
>
> *I wanted to write some lines to you just some time ago but I postponed it so long. You must forgive my delay, because there are a lot of things to look after and I have to do it all on my own. My children have all gone away, far away. It took a long time before I could get everything in order. I have received the picture and I thank you. I wish I had one of the boys for the company.*
>
> *Dear Anton* [sic], *I'm sending you 50 dollars in memory of your brother, my blessed husband. Everyone liked him, he was good to poor people, he couldn't see anyone go hungry. Above all, he was good to his family. He*

always worked hard. The last ten years he didn't work anymore because he left the business in order to find more time for each other.

Dear Anton, you say you are 9 years younger than Joseph. How old are you? I wonder whether Joseph really was 75 years old, he was always so fast on his feet and always held himself erect.

I don't know what advice I should give my nephew, Josef. Without knowing the language he can't do a lot and then everywhere is so crowded. If he's patient for 1 year or so until he has learned the language he'll stand more of a chance. Every commencement is difficult and it's like that here, too. You should have come when the children were small so that they could go to school.

The salary is not as good as it was 7 years ago, everything is more expensive. It needs a lot for the family to live: the wages are 3–7 dollars a day. Girls can earn 5–7 dollars a week for housework.

Not only the rich, but also the poor have cars. You don't see horses on the street anymore. People live too comfortable, easily, and luxuriously and then they moan about the hard times they have.

Dear brother-in-law, I send my regards to my sister-in-law and all the other relatives and remain your sister-in-law and Aunt Millie Prinster.

This was the last known correspondence with Joseph's European family until 1992, when Tayana contacted the family.

Millie carried on for another ten years. She immersed herself in Catholic organizations and was generous with donations. A few years after Joseph's death, her daughter Mary, now divorced with two small children, returned to La Junta and helped her mother oversee her twenty-eight rental properties.

In 1924, Millie loaned Paul $1,500 to buy a half-interest in a small grocery store at Fourth and Main in Grand Junction. It was also called City Market. She never dreamed that this small investment would pull all of her sons away from her like a powerful magnet. Only Edward, who had entered seminary in 1929, was not drawn to Grand Junction.[44]

On December 23, 1935, there was a fire in the building Millie owned and lived in. It held a drugstore and multiple apartments, one of them Millie's. She suffered lung damage from smoke inhalation and was in serious condition.[45] The smoke inhalation eventually brought on pneumonia, and Millie was admitted to the hospital four years after the fire and died from the lung damage. On January 19, 1939, the *La Junta Daily Democrat* made this announcement: "Short illness is fatal to pioneer Mrs. J.F. Prinster. After

Joseph and Millie moved to one of their apartments after leaving their home on Raton. *Courtesy of Dan Prinster and the Joseph C. Prinster family.*

a ten-day illness, Mrs. J.F. Prinster of La Junta died at her home 114½ Colorado Ave. She was 68."

The newspaper described her origins and her family members and then concluded, "The Prinster family was one of the most prominent in La Junta. Mrs. Prinster was affiliated with the Catholic Daughters of America and the Altar Society of St. Patrick's Catholic Church. She was also a member of the W.B.A. and was vitally interested in numerous charities and philanthropies."[46]

Millie's body was taken to the Peacock Funeral Home at 401 Raton. Millie's beloved family home now housed her body.

St. Patrick's had been the scene of so many previous Prinster events for half a century: baptisms, christenings, first communions, weddings and funerals. Millie's Requiem High Mass was celebrated by her son, Reverend Edward Prinster, and her nephew, Reverend Timothy Kroboth. Six other priests also assisted in the service.

Miriam Peckham, Millie's granddaughter by Mary Blevins, was eleven years old when her grandmother died. "All these people came to the house and told us what she had done for them," said Miriam. "There was a steady stream of mourners telling us that she was a very generous person."

Millie's funeral would be the last Prinster event to be celebrated at La Junta's St. Patrick's Catholic Church. With Millie's death, one era had ended and another was about to begin.[47]

Backstory Notes

Mary Prinster was the eldest and only surviving daughter of Millie and Joseph. After her marriage to Donald Blevins in June 1924, she and Donald had two children: John Donald Blevins Jr. on May 12, 1925, and Miriam Anna (Blevins) Peckham on May 21, 1927. After Mary and Don were divorced, Mary returned to live in La Junta. She had been trained in accounting and managed her mother's numerous rental properties there. She later moved to Grand Junction, where she died. Her daughter, Miriam, became a schoolteacher. After Miriam married, she and her husband adopted four children. Miriam died in Grand Junction on November 20, 2010.

Her brother, Donald, was inducted into the army in August 1943 as a private. Like his cousin Joe Prinster he fought in the Battle of the Bulge and later in battles in Normandy and St. Lo. He was awarded the Bronze Star in July 1944. He also was awarded the Commendation Ribbon, Combat Infantry Badge, the EAME Medal (European-African-Middle Eastern Campaigns) and five Bronze Stars. He was discharged on May 27, 1946, as a first lieutenant. Don returned to the army in 1950 and was sent to Korea. He won the Silver Star and the Purple Heart and rose to the rank of captain. At age twenty-six, Don was killed in action on October 14, 1951, two weeks before his orders for promotion to major were to come through.

PART II

THE BROTHERS FOUR

Paul H. Prinster: The Founder (1890–1956)

At six feet, five inches, Paul was the tallest of the Prinster brothers and the most outgoing. Everyone called him Slim. Born on July 6, 1890, he was the firstborn son of Joseph and Millie. Growing up in La Junta had not been easy for Paul. He and his brother Frank, two years his junior, relied heavily on each other to get through the turmoil and demands of their burgeoning family and the vicissitudes of their father's business. As a result, the brothers remained close friends throughout their lives.

At an early age, the brothers were taught the butcher's trade. While they were still in grade school, Joseph had put them to work in his slaughter, curing and retail businesses. Paul did not particularly care for school and was often truant. When his father took him out of school in the fifth grade to work full time, Paul was relieved.

Paul made such an impression on a young girl who attended grade school with him in 1901 that she wrote an essay about him years later. Her name was Josephine Alice Patterson, known as Jody (one day she would marry Paul's brother Frank):

> *When I was in the third grade, the school room was in the basement of the Columbian school building. La Junta being a growing railroad town had more families with children than places to teach. The adjoining room*

in the basement was for the fourth grade and the fourth grade pupils had to march through our room in order to get to theirs because we had the only outside door.

It was a warm Indian summer day with hot winds blowing over the prairie, rattling the windows, which were none too well constructed. Our teacher was cross, the pupils fidgety. Miss Hammond (Hammy) read a chapter of Dickens' Little Nell. All the students cried and the teacher wiped her eyes and blew her nose with a snort that equaled any man's because now was the touching scene when Little Nell died.

At that instant, a tall boy ambled through our classroom wearing what must have been his father's coat and in the lapel blazed a huge sunflower in all its glory. We little third graders forgot all the sadness of the story by now and watched Miss Beck, Paul's teacher, who had come in to consult with "Hammy." Her face resembled a chunk of putty. I sat near the door and heard her say, "Paul Prinster has been playing truant for three weeks. What shall I do?" Shortly Dr. Blaksley (the principal) arrived wearing his monocle, his gold tooth shining through his clipped moustache and his "I fawncy" every other word. The case of Paul was put before him but he must have thought Paul looked pretty big and not to be dealt with single handed, so he fingered his watch chain, dusted his waist coat and vest, smoothed his striped trousers and left to "Fawncy" somewhere else.[48]

By the time he was a teenager, Paul had become a skilled butcher and meat cutter, and both he and Frank were already managing their father's slaughtering, curing and grocery businesses.

On April 12, 1912, Paul married Carrie Palmer, a young lady from Santa Fe, New Mexico. The twenty-two-year-old Paul had met her in Swink at his Uncle Joseph Kroboth's home (Millie's younger brother). Carrie was Joseph Kroboth's sister-in-law. The Reverend Felix Dilly married them at St. Patrick's Catholic Church in La Junta, with Paul's brother Frank serving as best man and his sister Mary as Carrie's bridesmaid.

The *La Junta Tribune* took note of the wedding: "Only near relatives of the contracting couple were present. The wedding was a surprise to friends and relatives but cupid seems fond of springing surprises on everyone this spring." The paper went on to describe Paul as the oldest son of J.F. Prinster, saying, "He is an excellent young man of sterling qualities. Miss Palmer is an orphan and has made her home for two years past with her sister, Mrs. J.D. Kroboth of Swink."[49]

Paul and Frank in front of Prinster's Market in La Junta. *Author's collection.*

The couple rented a small apartment from Millie and Joseph in the Bradish Addition. Two years later, on July 4, 1914, their first child, Paul Joseph Prinster, was born. Not long afterward, on May 11, 1916, Carrie died. The attending physician gave the cause of death as "Wood Alcohol Poisoning, contributing to insanity of pregnancy."[50]

Apart from the statement on the death certificate, little is known about the circumstances of Carrie's death. The *La Junta Tribune* reported on Sunday, May 13, 1916, that "Mrs. Paul Prinster died Wednesday night at 11 o'clock at the Valley hospital after an illness of only a few days. Her sudden death came as a shock to her bereaved husband and other relatives as well as her many friends in this city." Paul was now a widower and responsible for the care of his two-year-old son.

Millie stepped in and took charge of Paul Jr. so that his father could continue to run the slaughter operation for Joseph. Shortly after Carrie's death, Paul and Frank decided to purchase the business from their father.[51] Paul chose to operate the slaughterhouse operations, and Frank ran the retail store on Colorado Avenue near the center of the town of La Junta.[52]

This change of ownership made it possible for Joseph to retire at the age of sixty-six.

During the next year, Paul met a young woman living in Rocky Ford. Her name was Edna Lampson. Paul and Edna were married on August 19, 1919, at St. Patrick's by Reverend Joseph M. Desaulniers. The witnesses for the couple were Paul's brother Leo and his wife, Freda. There was no mention of the marriage in the newspaper, and it is not known whether Paul's parents or Frank and his wife, Jody, were present. Paul and Edna had one child, a daughter named Billie May, but their marriage ended in divorce after a few years.[53]

In the meantime, Joseph used his retirement years to travel with Millie. Their favorite destination was Glenwood Springs, Colorado. This lovely mountain town could be reached easily by rail from La Junta. The surrounding mountains reminded Joseph of South Tyrol, and he and Millie enjoyed the hot springs there.

On one journey in 1919, they traveled west to Grand Junction, and both were impressed by the grandeur and scenery of the Western Slope. Joseph saw the potential for developing a business in this growing town. When the couple returned to La Junta, Joseph told Paul and Frank about Grand Junction. He said, "If you boys all stick together and go over there to Grand Junction and get into business, you can make a real thing out of it."[54]

Joseph was serious enough about the prospects in Grand Junction that he wrote a letter of inquiry to the Grand Junction Chamber of Commerce shortly after his return to La Junta. On Saturday, March 6, 1920, the *Daily Sentinel* reported that chamber of commerce secretary W.D. "Dent" Ela received a letter from J.F. Prinster of La Junta, saying that he will be in Grand Junction soon to talk of plans to build a small meatpacking plant in the city.[55]

In about 1919, Paul and Frank sold the slaughterhouse business and Prinster's Market in downtown La Junta. Joseph and Millie were traveling and seeking other opportunities for their sons in Grand Junction and Albuquerque. On September 19, 1921, the boys opened another market at 116 West Second Street in La Junta and named it City Market. They operated it until 1923 with a great deal of success and customer loyalty. And then in 1923, the *Daily Democrat* announced in bold type, "City Market Changes Hands."[56]

By 1923, Paul and Frank had decided to sell their business because they could see that things were changing in La Junta. The Santa Fe Railroad was moving its operation and management to Pueblo, which would have an adverse effect on the town. Some of the shops, facilities and management were also moving. A chance to sell their business arose, and they seized the opportunity. They sold City Market to A.E. Marsh and B.A. Freed, two businessmen from Rocky Ford, Colorado, who knew the meat and grocery business. The *Daily Democrat* reported, "The Prinster boys have been connected with this kind of business for many years in La Junta and have built up an excellent trade by their square dealings and business methods. They know the meat game from top to bottom and are now planning on opening up a packinghouse in La Junta if they receive the proper encouragement from the people in the vicinity. They have a proposition to embark in this kind of business in Albuquerque, New Mexico, where it is understood that the city has offered them a site and free water."

The offer from Albuquerque failed to materialize, and it is not known whether the brothers received the "proper encouragement" from the people of La Junta. But their business had sold, and Paul, for the first time in his life, was footloose and fancy-free. But it might be more accurate to say that Paul was at loose ends. His second marriage had ended in divorce, and he had two children to support. He and Frank did indulge themselves by each buying three-carat diamond rings. Frank's ring ended up on his wife Jody's finger, and Paul's eventually became an engagement ring for his third wife, Goldie Ridgeway.

Goldie was divorced from her husband, an engineer on the Santa Fe Railroad. Although Catholic, Goldie did the unthinkable as far as the church was concerned: she divorced her husband after learning that he had been cheating on her for years. The couple had one daughter, Barbara Jane. Paul was smitten with the attractive young Goldie, and he really loved Barbara Jane. But because both Goldie and Paul were divorced, they could not participate in the sacraments if they remarried. In other words, they would be excommunicated. Goldie told Paul that she would consider marrying him only if they moved away from La Junta. Her reason? "Too many Prinsters run things in La Junta."[57]

Millie must have liked Goldie because she hosted a lovely party for her before Paul left for Grand Junction. The only family members not in attendance were Frank and Jody. Jody was appalled that these two divorced people were getting married, thus becoming excommunicated and not being able to be married in the eyes of the church. They were certainly going to hell. Oddly enough, Jody held Goldie solely responsible for this "mortal sin" but not Paul.

Paul and Goldie after they moved to Grand Junction. *Courtesy of John H. Prinster.*

After selling City Market in 1923, Frank chose to stay in La Junta and partner with Leo in his pool hall and barbershop, but Paul was ready to seek new opportunities. As a youth, Paul had very little money, and the proceeds of the sale of the La Junta City Market left him financially well off for a young man of that day and age.

Now thirty-three years old, he bought a flashy 1922 red Buick convertible. Despite rough roads and the lack of highways, Paul headed west. His first thought was California, but he remembered his father's prophetic advice to check out Grand Junction ("If you boys all stick together and go over there to Grand Junction and get into business, you could make a real thing out of it"). His first stop was indeed in Grand Junction.

When Paul arrived, he found that he was immediately welcomed. People were impressed with this tall, charming young man with an easygoing manner and a penchant to engage in friendly conversation with anyone from a janitor to the bank president. He was entertained by various people in the community, who encouraged him to stay, and so he did.[58]

Paul had no trouble finding employment. He took a position with Piggly Wiggly, a supermarket chain in southern and western states with one store in Grand Junction. He was immediately made manager of the meat department. Once Paul had a job, he wrote to Goldie advising her to bring her mother and Barbara Jane and meet him in Glenwood Springs, where they married in the fall of 1924. They purchased a home at Sixth Street and North Avenue in Grand Junction that Paul put in Goldie's name. They later built a home at 1225 Ouray and occupied it for the next twelve years.

Paul's son, Paul Jr., age ten, decided to stay with Millie and Joseph after his father's marriage, while Billie Mae had gone with her mother after the divorce and remained estranged from her father for many years.

Grand Junction was expanding, and so was Piggly Wiggly. On April 30, 1924, the *Daily Sentinel* announced a downtown business expansion. William Buthorn and his associates had purchased space downtown and announced there would soon be another business block and a second Piggly Wiggly store built there. The new business block was to be located at the northeast corner of Second and Main Streets, directly north of the La Court Hotel. The new, modern Piggly Wiggly store, with an up-to-date meat market, would be operated by Paul Prinster. Paul placed an order for equipment including an extensive refrigeration plant.[59]

However, the new Piggly Wiggly was not to be—at least not a second store with a meat shop run by Paul—so Paul followed other plans. Two years before the new business block announcement in 1922, a Grand Junction resident, Adam Booker, had bought into a business at Fourth and Main Streets. The business was called City Market, and Booker's partner was a man named Hill. According to Booker, when Joseph Prinster had come to town looking for business opportunities for his sons, the two businessmen had met. After they talked, Joseph returned to La Junta and told his sons to consider buying Booker out.

In the brief time that Paul was with Piggly Wiggly, he also must have contacted Adam Booker. They reached an agreement for Paul to buy out Booker's partner, Mr. Hill. Paul then borrowed $1,500 from his mother and purchased Hill's interest, becoming partners with Booker.[60] Paul now had a start with his own business but wanted to purchase the whole enterprise. He needed his brother Frank. Paul began calling Frank on a regular basis, trying to persuade him to join him in the Grand Junction City Market. Frank was hesitant, but Frank's wife, Jody, finally made the decision to take him up on Paul's offer.

In the meantime, Paul and Goldie settled into a happy life together. Paul doted on Barbara Jane and indulged her and her mother in every way. After they moved into the elegant home on Seventh and Grand that had been built by the now-deceased Dr. Heman Bull, Goldie entertained often. Whenever Father Edward (Paul's brother) visited, she would host gatherings of family and friends to hear him play the piano in the music room. The only ones not in attendance were Frank and Jody. Jody's animosity toward Goldie continued, and when Goldie gave birth to John ("Jack") in 1930, Jody

Paul and Goldie's home at Seventh and Grand Avenue in Grand Junction. *Photo from* Grand Valley Magazine.

referred to Jack as their "bastard" son because she didn't consider his parents married.

Over time, Leo also began to disapprove of Goldie, but not for the same reason. He thought her silly and extravagant, especially after she started buying new furniture, as he said, "every three months." She tossed out the old or gave it away and then completely redecorated, according to Leo's daughter, Penny. "My father believed women belonged in the kitchen waiting on their husbands and not making a spectacle of themselves," she said.

None of this seemed to bother Paul. Jack remembered growing up in a very happy home filled with laughter and fun. Jack adored his mother and Barbara Jane and was fond of Paul Jr., who was seventeen years older.

Jack recalled a time when he was eight. It was during the Great Depression, and there were many hobos around. Two of them knocked on their door one morning wanting to work for a meal. They were dark-skinned men, and they frightened Jack, who had never seen a black man before.

This didn't faze Goldie. Her big home on Seventh and Grand had numerous windows, so she told the men if they washed all her windows, she'd feed them breakfast. They did an excellent job, so Goldie fried several pounds of bacon, two dozen eggs and a big serving of fried potatoes. They ate every bite. As they left, Goldie said that she'd find more work for them if they came back to Grand Junction. One month later, one did return. His name was John Simms. After Goldie talked to Paul about hiring him, Paul put Simms to work at their new store as a janitor. He stayed with City Market until his retirement and became a good friend to the family. Jack grew to love John because he could fix anything. If Jack wanted something made, John made it. Jack and his family attended John's big Fourth of July barbecue every year. Jack remained close friends with John and his family.[61]

At age twelve, Jack started working at City Market as a bag boy, just as his cousins had done, but Jack wasn't happy in the Grand Junction schools. When he was ready to attend high school, his parents sent him off to the very prestigious Phillips Academy in Andover, Massachusetts, a residential prep school established in 1778 and known for its academic excellence. Jack said that there were never more than eight students in his classes, and he described those four years as the best experience of his life. After he graduated, he returned to Grand Junction and worked for his father and uncles in their ever-growing enterprise. When his father, Paul, died in 1956, a family upheaval occurred that had far-reaching effects—not only on Jack's future, but the future of City Market as well.

Frank J. Prinster Sr.: The Peacemaker (1892–1975)

On a hot September morning in 1904, while La Junta's children trooped off to school, twelve-year-old Frank Prinster headed for work. He hadn't been inside a classroom for more than a year, and he wasn't too happy about it. Unlike his brother Paul, Frank liked school and was a good student, particularly in mathematics. But his father, Joseph, had run into financial difficulties a year earlier and had withdrawn his sons from school to work for him full time. Paul had been thirteen and Frank only eleven. Joseph's decision had provoked a heated discussion with Millie, who knew that Frank liked school. She didn't want him to quit in the fifth grade, but the needs of the family business gave Joseph the better argument, and he had prevailed.

Slender and tall for his age, Frank was beginning to look a lot like his father. Frank had Joseph's black hair and brown eyes and, like him, would grow into a tall, broad-shouldered man with rugged good looks. All of the Prinster boys grew to be six feet or more. Paul, the oldest, reached six feet, five inches; Frank was six feet, two inches; and Leo, the "shrimp," stood only six feet tall. They were known in La Junta as those "big Prinster boys."

On that morning, Frank entered the Prinster's Market at 119 Colorado Avenue. A large ad that ran daily in the local newspaper described his family's business as "J.F. Prinster, dealer in fresh and salt meats, poultry, oysters, and fresh vegetables in season."

Frank greeted his father, who had arrived much earlier. Joseph asked him to unpack some crates, so Frank donned his apron and went to work. The town was relatively still at that time of day. Children were in school, and the passengers from the departing train had dispersed and vanished into the dusty, quiet streets.

Frank had unpacked one crate and started on another when the bell jingled on the front door. He looked up to see a stranger enter. Just another drifter passing through, he thought. The young man was slightly built and stood maybe five feet, eight inches. He wore a dusty shirt and pants, broken-down boots and a large sweat-stained hat. Frank also noticed a pistol affixed to his hip by a large leather belt. To Frank, the stranger appeared desperate and threatening. As the man took a few steps inside the store, Frank shot a glance at his father. For a few seconds, the three men measured one another. And then Joseph moved quickly to the butcher's block, wrapped his hand around a meat cleaver, raised it high above his head and slammed it down hard on the block. Then he yanked it out and raised it again, a fearless glint in his eyes. The drifter got the message. He stepped backward, opened the door and ran down the street into a whirl of dust. Father and son sighed with relief. Joseph said nothing more about the incident and went back to work, but Frank never forgot his father's bold move that morning.[62]

Unlike his outgoing and impulsive brother Paul, Frank was shy, stoic, contemplative and often indecisive. He took time to think things through before acting. Despite his temperament, Frank learned to buy and sell products, calculate costs versus profits, set up attractive displays and carry on polite small talk while dealing with customers. There wasn't much Frank and Paul couldn't do in the business. Their father taught them how to greet customers, get the items they needed and tally up the bills. The boys also knew how to price items, and both were learning to be skilled meat cutters.

In those days and in their store, there was no self-service. Customers would step to the counter and tell Frank what items they wanted to buy. He would go to the shelf or storage room in the back of the store, get the items and bring them to the customers at the counter. Frank had been doing this part time and after school since he was ten years old.

For the next eight years, Frank and Paul continued their apprenticeship with their father. Although their formal education had ended, it was replaced

Frank Sr. (left) worked with his father in Prinster's Market at 119 Colorado Avenue, La Junta, circa 1906. *Author's collection.*

by the knowledge of how to run a successful business. Any graduate of a business school would have envied such training, and it would serve the brothers well in the years to come.

Their father was pleased enough with Frank's progress that he promised he would let him manage the store on his own one day. Two years later, at age fourteen, Frank was doing just that. Paul, in the meantime, had become proficient in the meat-processing end of the business.

Frank opened the store in the morning and closed it at the end of the day. He was careful to avoid any unnecessary risks when it came to his own or his family's assets, but he did have one vice. Frank loved gambling in card games, and he was good at it. Anything that involved numbers sharpened his wits, and he shrewdly calculated the odds and used this skill to his advantage. Later, his own eldest son, Frank Jr., in his essay "History of City Market," would write, "Frank was the second-oldest brother and not as flamboyant as his brothers Paul and Leo. He was the quiet one, the cement that kept the organization together. As in any family-run business, things do not always go smoothly. In this instance, because of the volatile personalities of his brothers, Frank seemed to be the peacemaker."

In 1917, Paul and Frank were in their early twenties and ready to take over the business entirely. They offered to buy out their father (probably with Millie's encouragement), and Joseph had enough confidence in them to agree. By then, Paul's first wife, Carrie, had died, and three years earlier, Frank had married a spirited little redhead named Josephine Alice Patterson, whom everyone called Jody.

Josephine "Jody" Alice Patterson (1892–1957)

The Gibson Girl look was the fashion in Jody's youth. Charles Dana Gibson's pen-and-ink illustrations set the beauty standard for American women and were considered the personification of the feminine ideal in the late nineteenth and early twentieth centuries. His images graced everything from ads to ashtrays. Jody was slender and pretty; stood five feet, seven inches; and had an hourglass figure. With her blue eyes, oval face and mass of red hair piled high on her head, she could have easily posed for one of Gibson's illustrations. Her husband, who remained in awe of her throughout their married life, was known to remark, "She didn't have that red hair for nothing."[63]

Jody was very much a Gibson Girl. *Author's collection.*

Jody was born in La Junta in 1892, the same year as Frank. When she was still a toddler, her family moved to Thoreau, New Mexico, where her father tried his hand at homesteading. Jody remembered living in a little one-room cabin with a dirt floor, and at age four, it was her job to wet the floor down and pat it afterward to keep it hard and free of dust.

Her father's homesteading effort wasn't successful, and the family moved back to La Junta, where she entered the third grade. Then she noticed two of the Prinster boys, Paul and Frank. When Jody's father died, Jody, her mother and two sisters moved back to New Mexico to live with her uncle, Wade Smith, who owned a large ranch. Her mother went to work as a postmistress in the nearby town of Crown Point. At the time Jody was to enter high school, her mother decided to return to La Junta.

Once again, Jody became acquainted with Paul and Frank Prinster, both of whom now took a keen interest in her, but it was the outgoing Paul who went after her first. Paul and Jody dated while she was still in high school, and although she found Paul amusing and a nice guy, she knew that he wasn't for her. It was Frank she kept her eye on. The indecisive Frank didn't move fast enough to keep Jody in La Junta after she graduated from high school. She went to Denver, moved in with an aunt and started work as a telephone operator. It was this aunt who awakened her interest in the Catholic Church. Jody converted to Catholicism and remained a fervent believer all of her life—her faith became *the* influence in her future family's lives. Her son Clarence, who became a Trappist monk known as Brother Nicholas, commented, "Whatever she saw in the Church, it was very deep in her."[64]

Jody made frequent trips back and forth from Denver and dated Frank when she was in La Junta. There was no question that they were falling in love, but Frank continued to dillydally, so Jody moved to San Diego for a while, taking another job as a telephone operator. Five years after her graduation from high school, she came home to find Frank ready to propose. She always knew that he would get around to it sooner or later, and she was ready to say, "I do." They were married at St. Patrick's Catholic Church in La Junta on June 22, 1914.[65]

The young couple moved into one of the apartments in the Bradish subdivision owned by her in-laws; Paul and Leo also lived there. It didn't take long for Jody to realize that she now had to contend with a very controlling mother-in-law. By the time Frank Jr. was born a year later, Jody had talked Frank into moving into their own apartment at 314 Fourth Street. At last they were out from under the nose of Millie—but not beyond her reach.

Millie chose to ignore the fact that her three oldest sons were now grown men and married. They were still her boys, and she had no qualms about directing their lives and those of their spouses. Her sons automatically adhered to her demands, even over the objections of their wives.

An example of this took place in 1920 after Millie received some communication from Europe. The thrust of these letters was that she might have an inheritance from a relative who had a large and very valuable piece of land in the region of her birth. She was told that in order to claim this inheritance, she or someone on her behalf had to travel to the area to claim it. Millie, now in her fifties, didn't want to make the journey, and neither did Joseph. But Millie was excited and determined. So she persuaded (insisted, more likely) her sons Leo and Frank to make the journey. Their wives, Jody and Freda, had a fit, but as usual, Mama prevailed.

The brothers, with the help of their father, who provided the necessary background information, applied for United States passports. Their passports were issued on May 27, 1920, and authorized them to travel to England, France, Spain and Switzerland for the stated purpose of "sightseeing and visiting sick relatives."[66]

They traveled to New York City and embarked on a ship to England. Years later, Frank and Jody's son, Joe, talked about the details of their journey:

> *They were on their way over there in a boat. And, of course, Dad got into a card game. He got to talking to this guy in the card game, and the guy asked why he was going to Europe. Dad told him the reason, and this guy said, "Oh, man, there's more of you dupes from out of the United States that get talked into that kind of stuff. You get these letters, and they tell you that all you got to do is bring a packet of money and you can buy whatever it is for cheap money, and then you'll be a big baron in a big castle. But that never happens. What happens is a gang of guys will end up killing you, and you'll never be heard from again. So don't go there. I know of at least three different guys who have gone there before, and they were never heard from again." So Dad and Leo figured that's that. It sounded logical. So they took the next boat and came back to the States.*[67]

The brothers returned empty-handed. Facing Millie's disappointment was the least of their worries. Jody, in particular, was so furious with Frank that she "wouldn't have anything to do with him," according to their son Joe. That's why there is a five-year gap between his sister Josephine's birth in 1917 and the birth of the twins, Marjorie and Mary, in 1923.

Prior to the European trip, Frank and Paul had sold Prinster's Market. A year after the European fiasco, Frank and Paul opened a new store, City Market and Grocery, at 116½ West Second Street in La Junta. Leo followed another business venture. He bought a pool hall and barbershop in La Junta.

Frank enjoyed giving Leo a hand in his business by keeping an eye on the card games and ensuring order in the house. He also maintained his own table, which became a source of cash for him. Things were still frosty at home, so Frank went to the pool hall after work, which meant that he was away from home all day and most nights. This just infuriated Jody even more. Then, of course, on Sunday, his day off, the family was practically ordered to attend Millie's family dinners at her lovely new house. It was not a happy time in Frank and Jody's home life.

Between 1923 and 1924, everything changed for the entire Prinster family. Paul and Frank sold City Market. Millie fell ill and ended up in a Denver hospital, followed by her sixteen-year-old daughter Lucille, who died shortly after an operation there. Frank and Jody's twins were born a few days after Lucille's funeral, and Paul, now divorced, left La Junta for Grand Junction.

Marjorie Prinster was a schoolteacher and an accomplished writer. *Courtesy of Dan Prinster and the Joseph C. Prinster family.*

When Paul had an opportunity to buy a half interest in the City Market on North Fourth Street in Grand Junction, he borrowed $1,500 from his mother and then began calling on Frank to join him. As usual, Frank had to think about it. After Millie sent Leo to check on Paul and the loan she had made, Leo returned to announce that Paul was struggling.

Paul continued to call, and Frank continued to think about it. Finally, one day, nine-year-old Frank Jr. was sitting in the kitchen when Uncle Paul called again. He overheard his indecisive father say, "Well, I don't know. Should we invite Leo?" There was a long silence on Paul's end, so Frank told Paul that Leo had a chance to sell the pool hall and might be interested in coming in with them. No decision was made then, but a few days later, when Paul called again, Jody answered the phone.

For several days, a hot, ferocious wind had been blowing through La Junta, and Jody's first question was, "What's it like in Grand Junction?" He told her that the people were nice and the weather and surrounding area were beautiful.

She then asked, "Does the wind blow in Grand Junction?"

Paul, realizing a ray of opportunity, answered, "No, never."

Jody turned to Frank and said, "I'm moving to Grand Junction, and you can come if you want to." They packed up and departed soon afterward. Their granddaughter Ann, who spent a lot of time with Jody in later years, said, "Jody was so quick to accept Paul's request because she had been looking for a way to escape from Millie."[68]

Not surprisingly, Leo and Freda also moved to Grand Junction with them, and Leo joined the business a year later. In 1926, the three brothers bought out Hill and Adam Booker, and a year later, their brother Clarence joined the partnership.

These were Frank and Jody's happiest years. Five more children were born to them, and all eight children have fond memories of their loving parents. Their granddaughter Ann (DeOnier) Griffin remembered witnessing a great devotion between Frank and Jody:

> *They guided the moral upbringing of their children, she with her voice and he with "the look." Jody was firm-willed and had a strong personality. She was fiercely protective of her children, establishing a close, unique relationship with each child. Her home was always immaculate; the three meals she served daily* [with lunch and dinner rigidly adhering to Frank's work schedule] *are still remembered by her children. With eight children to corral and discipline, she kept an ironing cord* [a cord that plugs into the iron] *tied around her waist as a threat, though she rarely used it. Her discipline was usually laced with humor, and she loved it when her children teased her.*
>
> *On one occasion, her adult daughters were helping her clean out a closet and found an abundance of five-dollar bills on the top shelf. Jody explained that Frank gave her five dollars every morning in case she needed or wanted something. Over the years, it had amounted to quite a sum. So her daughters asked if there was anything she'd like to spend it on, and she said she'd always wanted a fur coat. So off to Denver she went to buy a fur coat, returning empty-handed. When her daughters asked her why, Jody, who had become rather stout in her later years, replied, "They all made me look like a big bear."*[69]

Son Clarence (born in 1927), who became the monk Brother Nicholas, at the Abbey of Our Lady of the Holy Trinity in Huntsville, Utah had additional memories of his mother. He lovingly referred to her as "the General." He wrote:

Mama had a unique sense of humor and related very well to kids. She really loved kids, and that was a good thing because there were always a lot of them hanging around and a lot of dirty clothes to wash.

Our house had a deep basement with steep stairs going down. That's where the laundry was. No spin-cycle or tumble-dry in those days. Every Monday morning, down she went to tackle dirty clothes for ten people. There was an old "monkey stove" to heat the water, an old brass boiler with a lid, a hand wringer, and a suction. It was that suction that woke me up every Monday morning…sluuuup. I don't know how many tons of wet clothes she carried up those stairs to hang out on the line to dry over the years, but over and above the noise of that old monkey stove rumbling and the tubs banging and that old suction slumping, you could smell the pies baking, and more than that, you could hear her whistling. She could really whistle: popular songs, all kinds of arias, classical music, symphonies, and famous operas. We could hear her whistling all over the house, and we loved it.[70]

Although Frank's outward demeanor was quiet and calm and there are no family stories of temper displays from him, this didn't mean that he was without strong feelings and the ability to act on them. While living in La Junta, Frank displayed a deep feeling of protectiveness toward his father, especially when Joseph became elderly.

Joe, Clarence and Teo Prinster were close as brothers all their lives, circa 1932. *Courtesy of Dan Prinster and the Joseph C. Prinster family.*

Frank and Jody purchased their first home at Eighth and Grand Avenue in Grand Junction. *Courtesy of Dan Prinster and the Joseph C. Prinster family.*

During the years when Joseph was aggressively buying real estate in downtown La Junta, not only for Millie and himself but also for his sons, Frank often assisted him when dealing with bankers.

One day in 1920, Joseph, then sixty-six, was trying to explain to a banker in his thick German accent and broken English why he wanted to borrow money. The banker, using a voice dripping with disdain, said, "You crazy old kraut, just what the hell are you trying to do now?" Frank sat bolt upright, shot the banker a fierce look, took Joseph by the arm and marched him out of the bank. They never returned to that bank again. From then on, Frank held a deep suspicion of banks and bankers and rarely used banks for financing his own investments if he could avoid it.[71]

An example of Frank's stoic demeanor was shown at the new City Market in Grand Junction in the 1940s. The store was unusually busy one day, and the meat cutters couldn't keep up with the customers' demands. So Frank stepped behind the counter to help them out. When they ran out of hamburger, Frank said he'd grind some, and in his haste, he cut off two of his fingers. He emitted a short grunt, calmly shut off the grinder, reversed the blades, wrapped his bleeding hand in a white butcher's apron and walked himself out the back door to the doctor's office on Main Street. When he returned to work the next day, his hand wrapped in bandages, Paul took one look at his bandaged hand and jokingly said, "Well, we didn't charge extra for that hamburger, Frank. Is that OK with you?" Frank was much more careful from then on.[72]

Their daughter Margie wrote an essay about her family called "Mr. Prinster Goes to Lunch." It is a fine insight into the family dynamics. In one excerpt, she wrote, "At eleven o'clock, rain or shine, Frank senior follows his sons into the kitchen of his home calling out his familiar greeting, 'Hi, hi, hi, everybody,' as if he hasn't seen his family for a long time."

Margie goes on to describe how everyone shouted, "Hello, Pop." Frank would go into the front part of the house and ask, "Any mail from the private today?" He was referring to their son Joe, who was stationed at Fort Benning, Georgia. While Jody read the latest letter from Joe, the rest of the kids, mostly grown by now, helped put dinner together. The twenty-year-old twins might be frying steak and mashing potatoes, the boys were usually teasing everyone and sticking their fingers in the cake frosting and the radio was blaring. It often became so noisy that Jody closed the window so, as she put it, "The neighbors won't think a riot is going on." Finally, one of their sons calls, "Come on, Pop—food's on."

Margie's account continues:

> *With a look of utter contentment, Frank sits down to enjoy the ordinary course of the noonday meal with his family. After grace is said, everyone remembers that ten-year-old Lucille has not been called home from the neighbors yet. The mention of her name seems enough, and the youngest daughter bounds into the dining room leading an assortment of playmates, cats, and dogs. A perky twin jumps up to lead the uninvited guests out to the back yard with cake and milk until "Lukie" finishes her gravy and potatoes.*
>
> *While the twins and boys quibble over an extra dish of dessert, Lucille dashes out to rejoin her friends, the telephone rings for "Tweeb"* [Teo], *and their married son, Frank Jr., drops in for a chat.*
>
> *For another 20 minutes around the dinner table, Mr. Prinster relaxes in the chaos of the deafening radio, barking dogs, neighbors' children, telephone rings, and a tussle between Corny* [Clarence] *and Tweeb. Then at the stroke of 12, he brings the friendly squabble to an end, kisses his wife goodbye, reaches for his hat, and yells at his two sons, "Come on, boys, let's go."*[73]

Son Teo related his own fond memories of his father:

Like many families during World War II, the Prinsters worried about son Joseph as he prepared to leave with the army for Europe, June 1944. *Back, left to right*: Joe, Frank Jr., Clarence and Josephine. *Bottom, left to right*: Marjorie, Teo, Mary, Jody, Lucille and Frank Sr. *Author's collection.*

I do remember times when he would catch a shoplifter or a delivery man cheating him, and his wrath could be pretty scary. His patience with his family was something really special, and we have all seen some of that at one time or another. Along with that, he had a great sense of humor, because I know when Lukie [Lucille] *was a young brat of a sister, she would climb up on his lap, kinda for protection, which really didn't bother us too much until she would stick her tongue out at us. Boy, that would make me mad. Dad would just smile.*

This uneducated man from humble beginnings had a great deal of pride and exhibited his pride in the many things he did. He loved a nice car, not a fancy car, but a nice car, and he liked to keep it clean. He was fastidious in his personal habits and dressed pretty flashy. He loved his home, the store, and his accomplishments and the accomplishments of his children and wife. He enjoyed good food, a good boxing match, a good story, a song sung by

> *Eddie Arnold, and a good drink of Old Grand Dad bourbon. There was nothing really remarkable or great about Frank J. Prinster Senior, except how he lived his life. That made him a remarkable person.*[74]

The essence of Frank was calmness and patience. Displays of anger or strong emotions were quite rare. He exuded a demeanor of quiet strength. At the time of his death in December 1975, his sons received a letter from his longtime business associate, Cliff Baldridge, who wrote, "In all the years I knew your father, I never heard a harsh expression from him and can assume that his relationship with his family must have been one which gives you the utmost satisfaction in retrospect."[75]

Frank J. Prinster Sr. was regarded as the "Peacemaker" in the family. *Author's collection.*

Backstory Notes

The story of the trip to Europe has two different versions. The one related here was told by Frank's son Joseph C. Prinster. Frank's son Clarence (Brother Nicholas), in an August 2010 conversation, related that his grandfather, Joseph F. Prinster, had undertaken efforts to purchase property in an area near his birthplace in South Tyrol. He directed his sons Frank and Leo to travel to Europe to find out about the property. When they reached Europe (Brother Nick did not say which country or which city), they contacted the U.S. Embassy to get more information. They were supposedly told that the property sale, whatever its nature or location, was most likely a Mafia-type scam and were advised to abandon their efforts and head back to the United States. They did.

LEO G. PRINSTER: THE KINGFISH (1895–1985)

In the early hours of a cold December La Junta morning in 1912, Leo Prinster and his older brothers were awakened by their father's frantic shouts, "Boys, boys, get the horses, hitch the horses to the wagon. We have to get Andrew to the doctor!"[76]

Facing a howling wind and blowing snow, they whipped the horses into a frenzied gallop, only to arrive too late. Sixteen-year-old Andrew died that night in the doctor's office from a mastoid infection. The family was heartbroken at the loss of a second son, but Andrew's death had a particular impact on Leo. Only a year apart in age, Leo and Andrew were especially close.[77] Andrew's death would be the first of several events in Leo's life that would shake him to the core and start a bitter streak in his personality.

The third oldest of the Prinster boys, Leo was the antithesis of his brothers. Paul was easygoing and was charming to the janitor and the bank president. Leo would ignore the janitor and charm the bank president and other community leaders. Frank was quiet, more introspective and considerate of others, while Leo was narcissistic and blatantly ambitious.

The 1910 U.S. Census listed the occupations of Joseph's three oldest sons as butchers. By the 1920 census, the occupations of Joseph, Paul and Frank remained butcher, but Leo had become a proprietor of a pool hall. Leo was remembered as the pusher, the boss. Yet his brothers respected him and followed his direction, probably because of these very personality traits. Leo would one day propel them all into their astonishing success.

Like his brothers, Leo left school after the sixth grade and began working in the family business. By the time he was a teenager, he had become a skilled meat cutter. At nineteen, Leo was tired of the meat-processing and retail grocery business. He could see no future in it and so took a job as a switchman for the Santa Fe Railroad.

One cold and dark morning, after he had been on the job only a few months, he was walking across the rail yard when his foot caught in a power-driven switch. He struggled but could not pull it free. He watched in terror as a rail-mounted, hand-driven cart approached the switch. The men in the cart heard Leo's panicked shouts but were unable to stop in time. Leo's foot was crushed at the ankle.

Leo was treated at the Santa Fe Railroad hospital in La Junta. Surgical methods were crude and sterilization and infection control inadequate at best. His foot was amputated, but gangrene set in. To treat the gangrene, a second amputation was performed, then a third, which resulted in his losing his leg below the knee. Hospitalization and convalescence took more than a year. He was required to use crutches until he could be fitted with a crude wooden stump for a leg. From that time forward, Leo lived in constant pain.

After Leo moved to Grand Junction, he met a noted surgeon named Dr. J.U. Sickenberger, a rather prominent surgeon in his time, who suggested surgery to correct the handicap and eliminate the discomfort of the stump. The operation was successful, giving Leo much relief and allowing him to wear an artificial leg with relative comfort. Jack (Paul's son) remembers seeing Leo using a fingernail file to try and smooth out rough spots on his new prosthesis. Despite this, Leo contributed as much or more to the business as his brothers, and he became a good golfer and graceful dancer.[78]

During Leo's multiple surgeries and long convalescence in the hospital, a young nurse named Freda Rachael Wilson was put in charge of his care. She was the same age as Leo, barely twenty, attractive and slender, with light brown hair that she wore fashionably short. She had grown up in Kankakee, Illinois, and attended a nursing school in Chicago. After graduating from Robert Burns College in 1914, she accepted a position at the Santa Fe Railroad hospital in La Junta. Maybe it was fate.

She soon became a great source of comfort and support for Leo, and they fell in love. They were married at Lamar, Colorado, in December 1916. Freda quickly became a favorite in the family. Mary, Leo's younger sister, and Jody, Frank's wife, grew very fond of her. Freda and Goldie Ridgeway, Paul's

The operating room at the hospital in La Junta—a place Leo would never forget. *Courtesy of the Woodruff Memorial Library, La Junta, Colorado.*

third wife, became best friends. She also had a warm and close relationship with Millie. Initially, the newlyweds moved into the Bradish Avenue family compound, and Leo briefly went back to work in the family business.[79]

After Leo received a substantial settlement from the railroad for his accident, he and Freda invested in real estate and other businesses. They bought a number of lots in La Junta, and in 1920, Leo bought an interest in a business lot with his father, Joseph. A year later, Joseph transferred his interest in that lot to Frank, making Frank and Leo partners in what became a popular pool hall and barbershop. Frank's wife, Jody, was not happy about Frank spending his evenings in that establishment. In order to bring peace back into his marriage, Frank turned his half interest over to Jody, making her Leo's partner. Jody and Frank's granddaughter, Ann Griffin, commented years later that after that, Leo learned that he could not bully Jody.

By 1924, Leo had sold his business, and he and Freda moved to Grand Junction with Frank and Jody's family. They bought a house at 735 North Sixth Street in Grand Junction that Leo put in Freda's name. He then acquired an interest in another pool hall in downtown Grand Junction. When Paul and Frank decided to buy out Adam Booker's half interest in City Market in 1925, Leo sold his interest in the pool hall and joined them in the new business venture. Shortly after partnering with his brothers, Leo and Freda adopted a baby boy whom they named Andrew. Fatherhood added to Leo's mantle of "the boss" in the company with the mutual acceptance and understanding of his brothers.

Each brother assumed a specific role in the business. Paul concentrated on selecting top-quality livestock for processing and applying his knowledge of curing meat and making delicious sausages according to time-honored recipes developed in La Junta. Frank cultivated the restaurant business by calling on restaurants early every morning and quickly processing their orders, a business strategy used as a matter of course by today's top-performing corporations. These innovations were revolutionary at the time, and as a result, the meat-processing part of the business became the most profitable section of the store.

It was Leo, however, who had the vision of adding groceries to the inventory of what was primarily a meat shop, and he also insisted that all their transactions gradually be converted to "cash and carry." These moves had a profound impact on the business and were significant factors in its survival during the Depression years, when most businesses relied on credit customers.

Leo brought another important contribution to the business. Because of the loss of his leg, he was challenged by the physical work required in the grocery business. The long hours of standing, the lifting, the moving and pushing were not easy for him—although he gave his best. He soon assumed the bookkeeping, accounting and office responsibilities. He paid the bills, collected the accounts receivable and counted the cash. He became the "green eye-shade." He was conservative, tightfisted, hard-nosed and detailed. He made sure that the bills were paid on time and the receivables collected, and he counted every penny.[80]

In those early years in Grand Junction, Leo and Freda frequently hosted dinner parties and other entertainments in their home and developed a wide circle of friends. Although Leo worked long hours, he found time to pursue golf and enjoy social and business gatherings. Everyone loved Freda. She was a member of several social groups and was deeply involved with activities in the Catholic Church. Her presence was sought at dinner parties and events and in organizations. Freda suffered lingering effects from the great flu epidemic of 1918–19. She had developed a chronic sinus condition that eventually caused her death in 1932.[81]

Friends and family were shocked to learn of Freda's passing. No one, with the possible exception of Leo, knew of her suffering. She was never without a smile and never complained. Leo was devastated by her death, and the entire family mourned her. Millie, no stranger to the loss of a loved one, was equally affected. The *Daily Sentinel* reported that Millie arrived on Train No. 1 from La Junta to attend Freda's funeral service in June 1932.

One year after Freda's death, Leo remarried. He had met a pretty, petite blonde who had recently divorced Hardy C. Decker, Grand Junction's police chief from 1931 to 1935. Her name was Bernice Hatcher, and she had grown up on a farm in Loma, Colorado. They were married in Salt Lake City in the summer of 1933. Four years later, they adopted a daughter, Patricia, who was known as Penny. Freda forever remained in Leo's memory. Penny recalled how every year on the anniversary of Freda's death in June, Leo would pick a large bouquet of peonies from Bernice's garden and take them to the cemetery to place on Freda's grave.

Leo never attended church, although he considered himself a Catholic. Penny said that her father told her it embarrassed him to attend church because he couldn't kneel, and his artificial leg didn't fit in the pew. After he married Bernice, a divorced woman, he was considered excommunicated by church law. However, he saw to it that Penny went to church every Sunday. Penny said that after her father dropped her and her friends off, they would run off and do something fun. "I was always rebellious," she added.

Penny also remembered that Leo made frequent trips to Denver to have his prosthesis checked. "They coated his stub with chalk, had him walk around on his artificial leg, and then checked to see where the chalk rubbed on his stub. They'd make adjustments, and weeks later they sent him a new leg. It was attached to a big girdle that he wore around his waist, and the leg had air holes in it. He loved to entertain kids by letting them poke pins in his leg."

The brothers worked hard and prospered while remaining as close as brothers can be, but their families rarely socialized together except at Christmas. Jody had no use for either Goldie or Bernice, both divorced women. She was certain that they were going to hell. "My mother thought Goldie was a snoot," Joe later said of Jody. She also didn't like Leo. She felt that her husband, Frank, did all the work and Leo took all the credit.

Of the four, Leo was the high-stepper. He and Bernice frequently entertained leading members of the community, as well as sheep and cattle ranchers. They belonged to the Saturday Night Dinner Club at the Redlands Community Center, where they hobnobbed with Grand Junction's most prominent businessmen, politicians and members of the legal and medical professions. Leo was invited to serve on the board of directors of the First National Bank and became a charter member of the Bookcliff Country Club.

"My parents looked like Mutt and Jeff," said Penny. "She was itty-bitty and he was big." Penny remembered her parents as being a happy couple who had a wide circle of friends with whom they regularly socialized. Friends and business associates remembered their relationship differently. Leo was known to frequently criticize and belittle Bernice in their presence. She would react by shrugging and rolling her eyes as if it didn't bother her.

Leo could be very charming to the ladies. He liked women who knew their place (in the kitchen) and was gracious and outgoing to new acquaintances, especially those with high status in business and society. But Leo could also be extremely harsh and critical of his employees, business partners and especially the younger family members who worked in the business.

His daughter Penny, who went to work in their warehouse at age thirteen, remembered her father cussing out the workers. "I learned to cuss listening to him," she said. She added that her father was a very sharp businessman, and once you were his friend, you were his friend for life. "He served on the board of the First National Bank, and when they asked him to become president, he declined. He cited his lack of education. He was always embarrassed about that," she said.[82]

After the new City Market was built in 1939, Leo emerged as the boss. Everyone called him "Kingfish," after a character from the *Amos 'n' Andy* radio show. When anyone had a question or needed a decision to be made, they knew to go upstairs and ask the Kingfish. His rough edges and temper emerged from time to time, but he was the recognized leader, and his leadership was respected.

He always drove the latest model Cadillac. William Harris, a meat cutter at the Delta store, remembered Leo stopping at the store with a load of lamb. "He had three lambs in the trunk of his Cadillac and two lambs in the back seat," Harris recalled.[83]

Leo conducted as much business from his Cadillac as from his office. Glen Marler was working at the North Avenue store when Leo pulled up and asked him if he wanted to go to Durango as assistant manager. "He had me come out to his car, and we sat there and talked. I guess he didn't believe he should be in his office, he should be out working."

When Frank built a new house at Thirteenth and Chipeta on lots his wife, Jody, had bought at a big discount, Leo had to build one, too, at Twelfth and Gunnison. He paid full price to the Biggs & Kurtz Development Company and hired the same architectural firm, Atchison and Emery, that Frank and

Jody had used to build their home. Many years later, he also installed one of Grand Junction's first swimming pools at his home. Penny remembered looking out the window and seeing her dad and Uncle Frank in the swimming pool. The two typically took a swim after work in the summer. "The two of them looked so much alike," said Penny, "with their swim caps on. They would hold on to the side of the pool and talk and talk."[84]

On any business day in the new City Market, you would find the brothers together at work. Paul, tall and skinny, nicknamed Slim, would be dressed in a white butcher's smock and white butcher's hat, sitting on an egg crate in the back room smoking a cigarette and giving orders and advice. When giving orders, he'd point his long, bony finger to make his point and then spice his directives with a generous portion of butcher's profanity.

Frank, dressed in a white apron, white meat cutter's hat, shirt and tie, would be working at the counter in the back of the store, checking and

Leo took a lot of pride in his merchandising prowess. *Author's collection.*

Leo was a shrewd businessman and a leader in the community. *Author's collection.*

receiving deliveries and supervising the restaurant orders, or he'd be cutting meat for the sales case.

Clarence could usually be found in the front of the store supervising the checkout operations or stocking shelves. Leo, always dressed in a shirt, tie and business suit, would be in his office on the second floor, his eagle gaze watching the sales floor, or he'd be talking on the telephone. When he came out of his office, he could be heard before being seen, his presence announced by the uneven, thumping cadence of his wooden leg.

Although Leo only had a sixth-grade education, life had taught him as much as he needed to know. He became a shrewd businessman and a leader in the community. But behind Leo's intimidating manner was a considerable sense of insecurity that caused him to be verbally abusive and insensitive to family members and co-workers. Eventually, this would lead to his undoing in the family enterprise by being unseated as the Kingfish.

Backstory Notes

Stories about Leo's accident vary as to what happened and how. One version notes that Leo was not an employee of the Santa Fe Railroad but rather was walking across the rail yard late at night, perhaps returning from a party. He stepped on the rail as the power switch was closing, and his foot was crushed.

Another version holds that while at work switching cars, his foot was caught and an engine ran over his foot and crushed it. Leo's daughter, Penny, did recall her father telling how a hand cart ran over his foot after his foot had been caught in the switch and crushed it. She cannot confirm that Leo was actually employed by the Santa Fe Railroad.

The global mortality rate from the 1918 influenza pandemic has been described as the greatest medical holocaust in history and may have killed more people than the Black Death of the Middle Ages. It affected every corner of the globe and killed more people in twenty-four weeks than AIDS killed in twenty-four years and more than the Black Death killed in a century—approximately 25 million people died in its first twenty-four weeks.

Clarence F. Prinster: The Artist (1904–1997)

The youngest of the Brothers Four, Clarence shared similar traits with each of them. He was almost as tall as Paul and had his congenial personality. Like Frank, he was shy, considerate and thoughtful. He loved to dance and socialize just as Leo did, and like Leo, he was very civic-minded.

Just as his brothers did, Clarence worked in Prinster's Market in La Junta at an early age, but his experience in the meat-processing side of the business was limited. He never became a skilled butcher like Paul or an accomplished meat cutter like Frank and Leo. Clarence was the only one of the four who did not call himself a skilled butcher.[85]

Clarence and his older brother Edward, who became a priest, were the only sons of Millie and Joseph to graduate from high school and go on to higher education. Clarence attended Regis High School in Denver and graduated from La Junta High School. He went on to attend Barnes Business College in Denver, graduating in 1925. Afterward, Clarence was invited to join his brothers in their Grand Junction enterprise.[86]

He was twenty-one years old when he arrived in Grand Junction and moved in with Leo and Freda. He worked as a clerk for hourly wages, and soon his brothers acknowledged his skill in customer relations. Everyone liked Clarence, from his family members to the employees to the customers who sought him out. With his pleasant and helpful demeanor, Clarence was the diplomat on the sales floor and built a prized reputation for himself in his brothers' growing enterprise.[87]

Mary Roessler and Clarence Prinster on their honeymoon, circa 1933. *Courtesy of Fran Wilson Higgins.*

A few years after moving to Grand Junction, Clarence met an attractive young lady named Mary Roessler, who was attending Loretta Heights College for Women in Denver. Mary was the oldest of four girls who lived just a few blocks from where Clarence lived with Leo and Freda.

Clarence courted Mary for several years until he had saved enough money to get married. He and Mary tied the knot on September 6, 1933. It was to be an enduring and happy marriage that lasted sixty-three years. They adopted three children: Phillip and the twins, Ann and Susan. Clarence was not a disciplinarian. He was content to leave that chore to Mary.

By the time City Market No. 1 opened in 1939, Clarence had earned enough respect from his brother Leo that Leo granted him an interest from

Left: Mary and Clarence on their travels. *Courtesy of Fran Wilson Higgins.*

Right: Clarence, ever the artist, dressed the part for a Lion's Club carnival. *Courtesy of Fran Wilson Higgins.*

his own share in the family business, and Clarence added to this interest by buying shares in each new store that the brothers opened.[88]

In 1950, when City Market No. 2 opened on North Avenue, Clarence was made manager. But his heart wasn't in the business, and he proved to be less than brilliant at his new job. Since his teen years, Clarence had harbored a secret passion to be an artist, but he knew that it wasn't a practical ambition, especially in a family of butchers and meat cutters.

In midlife, Clarence became serious about painting again. He attended seminars and workshops and took classes to learn to paint. He displayed a natural talent early on, and as his dedication to art grew, so did his talent. He also became a gifted gardener. His artistic nature carried over into his beautifully tended yard.[89]

Like Leo, Clarence was civic-minded. He was on the board of the Colorado Society of Mental Health and was a lifetime member of the Grand Junction Lions Club, BPO Elks Lodge No. 575 and the Knights of Columbus No. 1062. In addition he was a founding member of the Mesa

County Art Association and the Colorado Center for the Arts, where some of his paintings are still in the permanent collection.[90]

After Clarence retired from City Market in 1969, he devoted himself full time to his art and his garden. He and Mary traveled to Europe once, but Mary did not enjoy traveling. When they were home, he entered numerous regional art shows, where he repeatedly won top honors. He was known for his landscapes, still lifes and modern abstracts in oil, watercolor and acrylic.

Clarence outlived all of his siblings, dying of natural causes at the age of ninety-two. None of his children or grandchildren pursued careers in the grocery business.

Edward C. Prinster: The Skiing Padre (1902–1956)

Handsome, outgoing, fun-loving, smart, talented, ambitious and dedicated, Edward Prinster embodied all the best traits of the Prinster family. He knew by age seven that God had called him to the priesthood.

He worked alongside his family members in his father's grocery and meat business until his graduation from La Junta High School. He then attended the University of Notre Dame in Indiana, specializing in business administration and music. In the fall of 1930, he entered St. Thomas Seminary in Denver to study for the priesthood. His ordination took place on May 22, 1937, in the Cathedral of the Immaculate Conception, officiated by the Most Reverend Urban J. Vehr, DD (per the ordination announcement sent out), bishop of the Diocese of Denver.[91]

And so began Father Prinster's nineteen years as a priest, dedicated to his church and his community. He left behind a lasting legacy for all who knew him.

Father Eddie is remembered for many things, and music was high on the list. No one knows when he learned to play the piano, but he became very proficient. While in seminary, he served as assistant choir director and organist for five years. During those same years, he also acted as organist at the Cathedral of the Immaculate Conception whenever his seminary choir sang there. He earned extra money by playing the piano at Denver's Blue Bird Theater as a prelude to the movies shown there.[92]

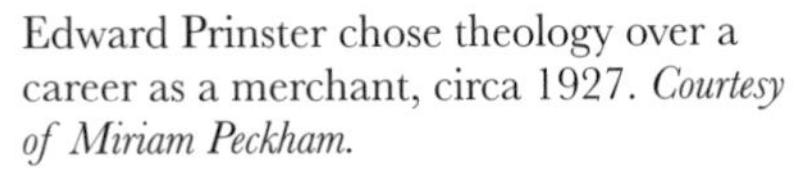

Edward Prinster chose theology over a career as a merchant, circa 1927. *Courtesy of Miriam Peckham.*

Father Edward Prinster at his ordination in 1937. *Courtesy of Miriam Peckham.*

He could play every kind of music and generously acceded to requests for certain tunes when he visited anyone's home. His visits to Grand Junction always occasioned a musical performance in the music room of his brother Paul's home, attended by family and friends.

An avid outdoorsman, Father Eddie spent his summers while in seminary helping the Right Reverend Joseph Bosetti, founder of St. Malo Camp and Retreat in Estes Park, train boys in the Catholic faith. They also introduced them to the joy of outdoor activities in the splendor of the Rocky Mountains. After his ordination in 1937, Father Eddie served as assistant pastor at St. Patrick's Church in Denver for two years.

In 1939, Father Eddie was appointed pastor of Steamboats Springs' Holy Name Catholic Church, and he also served the churches of nearby Mount Harris and Oak Creek—except that neither could be called churches in the traditional sense. The Holy Name Church in Steamboat was actually a large white frame home that had been converted into a place of worship, while Mass in Oak Creek was celebrated in the local mortuary, where parishioners knelt on the floor. Father Eddie's predecessor, Father Meyers, had tried for years to raise enough funds to build a church in Oak Creek, but it was Father Eddie who made it happen.

Construction of the Oak Creek Catholic Church began in 1940, one year after Father Eddie arrived in the area. It was completed in 1941 at a total cost of $6,500. The largest contributors were Mr. and Mrs. Martin Bieschke, who donated $1,500 and were given the privilege of naming the new church. Their choice was St. Martin's, a name that was used for the next fifty-three years.

Many smaller donations from locals and parishioners made it possible to pay off the church upon its completion in 1941. The church was dedicated in June 1942 by Bishop Vehr. Father Eddie donated six large candlesticks in memory of his parents.[93]

Six months before St. Martin's Church was dedicated, one of the worst mining disasters in Colorado history took place in Wadge Mine in Oak Creek. Thirty-four coal miners lost their lives on January 27, 1942, in an explosion of unknown origin. Four men, working near the mouth of the mine, escaped uninjured after hearing a blast and seeing smoke. It took the four survivors forty-five minutes to climb out of the air shaft near the mine office and report the explosion at 10:30 p.m. An emergency call brought rescuers, ambulances, morticians and miners' families from throughout the region to the scene in record time. Father Eddie was among the first to arrive.

With citizens working through the night with giant blowers, the mine's gas-laden chambers were finally blown out by midmorning of the following day, and Father Eddie rode with the first rescue team down into the deep, dark, smelly shaft of the mine.

What they found was grisly beyond belief. Charred, mangled bodies and body parts were everywhere, some without heads and most with their clothes blown off. It would take dental records and shreds of clothing to eventually identify the victims. After administering Last Rites, Father Eddie helped wrap the remains of these unfortunate miners in burlap bags and accompanied the first eight of them out of the tunnel. Throughout the day, he comforted the grieving families as they walked past the wooden slabs laid out in the Oak Creek morgue and tried to identify their loved ones. It took all day to retrieve thirty-three bodies. They never found the thirty-fourth body, and two of those they did find remained unidentified. The people of Oak Creek never forgot how Father Eddie compassionately comforted and prayed with them during their horrific ordeal.[94]

Father Eddie is also remembered for organizing the boys of his parish into a group fostering outdoor recreational activities. They were known as the Junior Mountaineers. In return, his boys taught him to ski. Skiing led to his playing a major role in the development of the Steamboat area

Father Eddie was known in Steamboat Springs, Colorado, as a "one-man chamber of commerce." *Courtesy of Miriam Peckham.*

as a major winter sports center. He took such a prominent role in all civic activities that he became known in Steamboat Springs as their "one-man chamber of commerce."

Father Eddie regularly encouraged his nephews to visit him in Steamboat Springs, something they all remember with great fondness. Tony Prinster, Frank Jr.'s oldest son, kept one of the letters his parents received in the 1950s from his uncle:

> *No doubt Tony has grown fonder and fonder of the city by now and he might not care about this hillbilly forsaken country anymore. You know the old adage, "out of sight, out of mind."*
>
> *We have a nice skating rink right across the street from me. The Kiwanis Club has charge of it, and besides a warming shack and night lights, there is continuous music being recorded for skaters.*
>
> *Did you see Collier's Magazine for this week? There is a nice article about Steamboat Springs in it.*
>
> *Hey, hey, I have been giving piano lessons these last several months. Yes, Mam, two pupils I have who wouldn't take no for an answer. I'm sure Tony is a Whiz by now...he has the talent and so he should be a Whiz on the piano. I have even improved a great deal myself.*

Must close and see what's cooking. Love and prayers for Daddy, Mommy, Tony, Tari, Tommy and Bernadette ("now daddy, I just made your bed, swept the floor, etc").

The Sage from the country,
"Brush"

P.S. my ping-pong table is sick from loneliness.

Father Eddie had begun to make plans to build a new Holy Name Church in Steamboat Springs to accommodate the expanding Steamboat population when tragedy struck on December 12, 1956. The headlines in the local paper announced:

FATHER EDWARD PRINSTER DIES AFTER FALL FROM ROOF WHILE MOVING SNOW; BODY FOUND EARLY THIS MORNING.

Father Edward J. Prinster was found dead this morning at Holy Name Parish residence where he apparently fell from the roof last night while shoveling snow. Mr. and Mrs. John Kimble noticed him lying on the front walk just below the steps at 7:25 a.m. He was dead at the time. The upstairs window of the house was open and a shovel was sticking in the snow on the roof. Father Prinster apparently fell on his head and there is evidence he struggled to reach the house after he fell.

Routt County coroner Howard Root attributed his death to a fractured skull.[95]

Two Solemn Pontifical Masses of Requiem were offered for him, one in Steamboat Springs and the other at the Immaculate Conception Cathedral in Denver. He was buried at Denver's Mount Olivet Cemetery. At the cathedral, then archbishop Vehr, who had ordained him as a young priest and who had dedicated his church in Oak Creek, expressed his admiration for Father Eddie. "Much good was accomplished by this friendly, cooperative priest in a largely non-Catholic community. He was a faithful missionary and a gentlemanly and kindly priest."[96]

PART III

THE SUPERMARKET EMPIRE

Grand Junction (1924–1939)

When Frank and Leo left La Junta for Grand Junction in 1924, the Western Slope was considered a remote destination. By then, Colorado's great mining boom had passed into history, along with the exploits of Colorado's early explorers, soldiers, mining tycoons, prospectors and cattle barons, and the state's economy had switched from dependence on gold and silver to agriculture and livestock.[97]

The automobile had just begun to penetrate the mountains, but the roads were primitive and more suited for stagecoaches and mule-driven freight wagons. The automobile was not an expeditious way to travel. The railroads offered a better way to move families to their destinations, so Frank and Leo hired a "Zulu car," the name given to emigrant cars by railroaders, to transport their families and all their possessions to the small town of Grand Junction.

Frank and Jody traveled in the Zulu car with their four children: Frank Jr. (nine), Josephine (seven) and the twins Marjorie and Mary (one). At the time, Jody was three months pregnant. Son Joseph would be born the following April in 1925 at the original St. Mary's Hospital. The entourage, including Leo and Freda, arrived in Grand Junction in October 1924.

For the first three months, the two families stayed in a hotel at Second and Main Streets. Frank and Jody rented two rooms to accommodate their larger family. Two months later, they purchased a two-story house at Eighth Street and Grand Avenue. Newlyweds Paul and Goldie had already bought a home in the 600 block of Gunnison, and in March 1925, Leo and Freda moved into a home at 735 North Sixth Street, just around the corner from Paul and Goldie. All three men put title and ownership of their homes exclusively in their wives' names.[98]

Frank immediately went to work with Paul at the small City Market that Paul owned with Adam Booker. Leo, for a short while, followed his previous career and acquired an interest in a pool hall on Main Street between Fourth and Fifth Streets.

In 1924, there were numerous neighborhood mom and pop grocery stores throughout town. Estimates at the time suggest that there were as many as fifty to seventy-five such stores within the Grand Junction city limits.

City Market, located immediately south of the alleyway and on the east side on North Fourth Street, north of Main Street, was on leased property with no more than a fifty-foot frontage and one hundred feet in depth. It was primarily a butcher shop selling meats, and there was nothing modern about it—no refrigeration other than iceboxes, no power meat saws or grinders and no electric cash registers. Across the street was the only chain store in town, Piggly Wiggly, and competition was fierce.

Leo, who in his younger years had tried to avoid the grocery business, decided a year later to join his brothers. He sold his interest in the pool hall and, together with Paul and Frank, bought out Adam Booker on August 3, 1926.[99] Their brother Clarence joined the business in 1926 and moved in with Leo and Freda until his marriage to Mary Roessler on September 6, 1933.

"From then on," as Leo would say in later years, "we worked like dogs." They worked long hours, 6:00 a.m. to 8:00 p.m. during the week and 7:00 a.m. to 10:00 p.m. on Saturdays. The store was closed on Sundays, but the brothers spent that day attending to book work and other details and preparing for the next week's business.

They had to grind hamburger by hand, which was a task for strong arms. Paul made sausages using old-world recipes that he had learned from his father. His excellent sausage was in such demand that it helped the small business stand out and grow. For a time, Paul maintained a smokehouse at a vacant lot on the corner of Fourth and Rood where he sold pork and smoked meats for bacon and sausage. Frank went out each morning to take orders from local restaurants, which he promptly filled and delivered. Because the brothers operated on a "pay as you go" philosophy, when the

Great Depression hit in 1929, they were not as affected as were most other businesses in town.

From the beginning, the brothers cultivated good relations with the farmers and ranchers in the Grand Valley. This served to help them grow the business rapidly and survive the Depression years. Paul, in particular, exhibited a special knowledge of the cattle and hogs produced in the valley, and he had a talent for knowing what to buy. The brothers followed a practice of buying their livestock and produce locally, then issuing as payment either cash or credit for purchases in their store. They were known to be fair and honest in their dealings with these local producers, thereby creating a partnership that benefited the brothers as well as the community.[100]

During those early years and throughout the Depression, it was not easy to gain access to the markets in the eastern or western parts of the nation. This local partnership arrangement provided City Market with a source of fresh products and provided a market and a source of cash for the farmers and ranchers.

The business grew steadily, and the brothers expanded the tiny storefront building several times along the alley

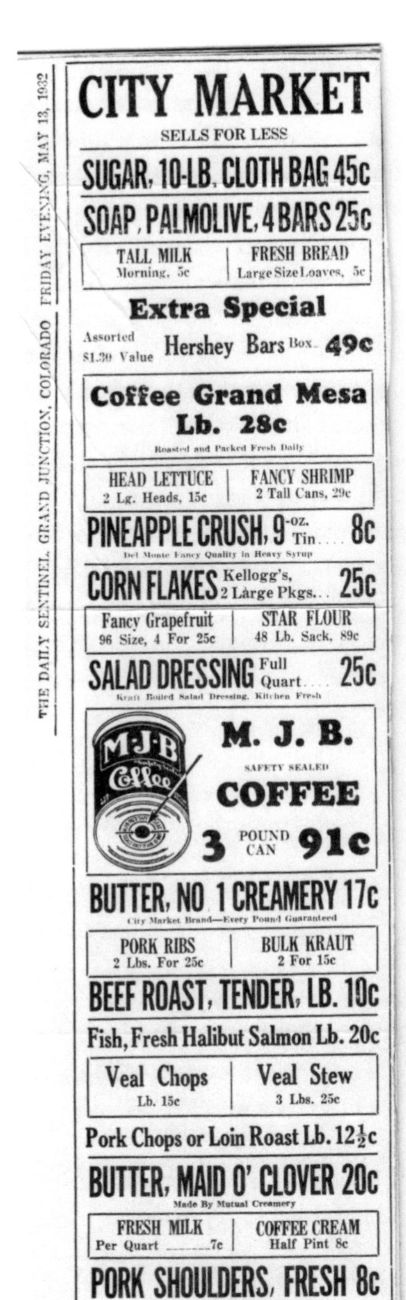

City Market ran weekly ads showing competitive prices during the banner wars. *Author's collection.*

on the north side of what was then the Mesa Drug store. In 1929, they did a complete remodel of the North Fourth Street location, but they were always looking for more space.

According to family lore, Frank was the financial manager of the business. He took charge of all the money decisions. He oversaw the wages paid out, the partnership distributions and the firm's investments. As manager of the firm's capital, Frank invested the profits and surplus in stocks and bonds, working with various brokers. From 1926 to 1929, his stock market investments did very well. In late October, the brokers suggested that the market was too high and expressed their concern. Frank was also uneasy about the stock market levels and agreed that they should sell all their stocks.

Nine days later, on October 29, the stock market crashed. Right before the event, Leo had been arguing with Frank to put more money into the stock market. After Frank told him he had liquidated their stock, Leo was furious. It led to one of the only serious conflicts between Frank and Leo. When the crash hit, Frank said nothing more about it, and neither did the subdued Leo. The proceeds were put into post office bonds that paid only 4 percent per annum, but they were safe.

The original City Market, located on North Fourth Street, Grand Junction. The store was purchased from Adam Booker in 1924. *Author's collection.*

Another Depression-era challenge involved the script issue. During the Depression years, some local government agencies paid their employees in script instead of cash. These scripts were basically promises to pay the salary of the employees "in the future." Teachers, especially, were paid by this means. The brothers decided to accept script in exchange for groceries. It became a great success with teachers and built a strong loyalty with their customer base.

City Market accepted the script at a small discount of 5 percent. Frank was in charge of collecting and accounting for the script, which he stuffed in coffee cans, hid in drawers and locked in closets. Since the script was backed by the county government, when they were redeemed in 1937 and 1938, the brothers were able to recover their investment, plus a small profit.[101]

Despite the Depression, the Brothers Four were enjoying prosperity because of the long hours and hard work. In 1936, Paul and Goldie, along with their daughter, Barbara Jane, and their son, Jack, moved into an elegant home at Seventh and Grand originally built by Dr. Heman Bull. Now with

The meat department in the original City Market. *Left to right*: Paul Sr., Paul Jr., Frank Sr. and Clyde Cording, circa 1932. *Author's collection.*

eight children—Clarence, born in 1927; Leo (Teo), born in 1928; and the youngest, Lucille, born in 1933—Jody informed Frank that they, too, needed a larger home.

In October 1937, Jody bought three and a half lots in the new Lincoln Park addition to the city of Grand Junction with the street address of 1302 Chipeta. She paid $400 for the lots. Frank questioned why so many lots. He thought that one or two would have been adequate, but Jody was determined to build a fine house with plenty of room inside and out.[102]

A local builder recommended the Denver architectural firm of Atchison and Emery. Jody hired it and then set out her specifications and requirements. The firm designed a beautiful colonial-style home for her. The house was completed in April 1938, and the family began the task of moving in. Joe, Frank's second son, was thirteen years old and remembered the event. It was Easter weekend, Good Friday. Jody was occupied with services and activities at the church. She left Frank in charge of getting the family fed that evening in her absence. Being in the meat business, Frank brought home a cooked ham for dinner. He made ham sandwiches for Joe and his siblings. Being Catholic and this being Good Friday, Joe was concerned. He explained to his father, "We are not supposed to eat meat."

Frank looked at Joe momentarily, then quietly and calmly replied, "It's OK, I talked to God."[103]

Their new home comfortably accommodated their twins, Joseph, Clarence, Teo and Lucille, as well as Frank Jr. when he was home from college and Josephine when on vacation from nursing school.

Leo, who had an adopted son, Andrew, and an adopted daughter, Penny, also wanted to build a new home. He hired the same Denver architectural firm that Frank and Jody had employed. In December 1937, he purchased three lots in block one of the Lincoln Park additions from J.C. Kurtz for $500 and began construction on his home at the corner of Twelfth and Gunnison.

The brothers knew that they needed to expand their business. Their original little store was bursting at the seams. They began buying lots adjacent to the original store.

For fifteen years, between 1924 and 1939, the brothers had nurtured their business, raised their families, built new homes and acquired capital. Their little neighborhood store was too small, and serious new competition had moved in. By 1939, Piggly Wiggly had been acquired by Safeway statewide. This was a new chain that would remain their major competition for the next seven decades. In response to these forces, the brothers moved to build

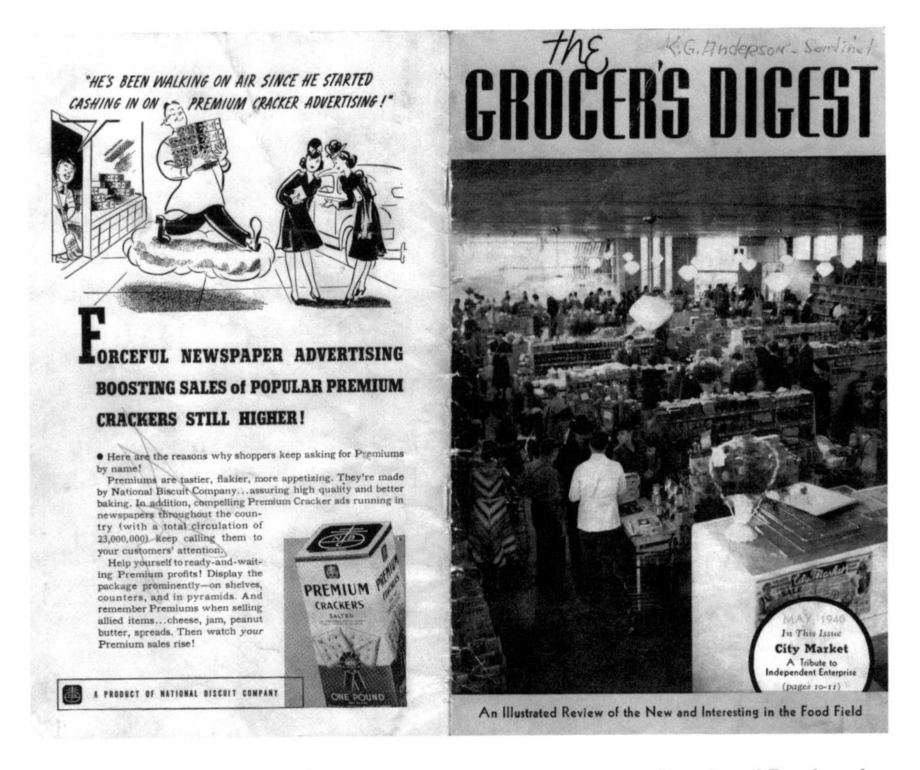

A magazine spread showing the interior of the new City Market at Fourth and Rood on the grand opening day in 1939. *Author's collection.*

a new store that, in time, would set the standard for retail grocery stores throughout the state.

In November 1938, the brothers acquired four lots from Pearl Warren for $1,750 per lot, and in January 1939, they bought two corner lots from Biggs & Kurtz for $6,000 each. These lots were located on Rood Avenue at the Fourth Street intersection. Cash was paid, no financing, not only for the land but also for the $75,000 store construction itself. After Biggs & Kurtz removed its equipment from the property, construction began immediately.[104]

In September 1939, to much acclaim, not only the biggest grocery store on the Western Slope but also, for a time, the largest supermarket in all of Colorado opened its doors. It was called City Market, the first of the new stores that the brothers would establish in the necklace of cities and towns that linked southwestern Colorado.[105]

The opening of the new City Market was not only a giant leap forward for grocery retailing in western Colorado, but it was also the threshold point for the next generation of the Prinster family to enter the business. Prior to the opening of that City Market, the family enterprise was owned, operated and dominated by the three original brothers: Paul, Frank and Leo. They provided the capital, developed the business strategies, met the payrolls, worked the long hours and provided the direction that enabled the small store acquired from Hill and Booker to grow into a modern-day supermarket.

Between the years 1928 and 1939, as the younger family members were growing up, they were introduced to the requirements of the grocery business. After Clarence, the youngest of the four brothers, moved to Grand Junction in 1926, he worked for hourly wages. Paul's oldest son, Paul J. Prinster (Paul Jr.), moved to Grand Junction in 1932 after graduating from high school and worked with his father in the meat and butchering operation. Frank's oldest son, Frank Jr., originally wanted to become a doctor and had graduated from Creighton University in Omaha, Nebraska, with a degree in chemistry. But romance entered the picture, and he decided instead to get married. He was persuaded to join the family enterprise and initially worked in the produce operations for weekly wages.

Clarence celebrates with his nephew Frank Jr. at his Creighton graduation in 1938. *Courtesy of Dan Prinster and the Joseph C. Prinster family.*

One month after the opening, the three brothers took the first steps toward an ownership change. Interest in the land and building at the Fourth and Rood site was given to their younger brother, Clarence, and the two oldest sons. The three brothers owned the business in equal thirds. Paul gave Paul Jr. a small part of his interest, Frank Sr. transferred a portion of his interest to Frank Jr. and Leo transferred to his brother Clarence a part of his ownership.[106]

Years later, Frank Prinster Jr. summarized the three cornerstones of the business philosophy to which the brothers and their descendants adhered: invest in the latest equipment and insist on a super-clean store, sell on cash-and-carry basis (no credit) and price groceries and meats cheaper than anyone else.[107]

These tenets were the anchor points of their business plan that had carried the brothers from La Junta to the small store on North Fourth Street in Grand Junction to the modern-day City Market and its ultimate dominance across the Western Slope.

Backstory Notes

Frank Prinster Sr.'s sons attributed to him the financial-management talent that enabled the business to prosper and grow between the years of 1924 and 1939. He invested part of the profits and surplus funds from the business in the stock market for additional growth and profits. They attributed to him the shrewdness to have liquidated the funds in time to avoid the crash of 1929. Frank reentered the stock market around 1934. For a man with no more than a sixth-grade education in La Junta, Colorado, his sense for numbers and finance was remarkable. He employed the services of four or five stock-and-bond brokers and advisers in Denver and Pueblo, Colorado. His journals show that he used Amos C. Sudler and Company in Denver, Sullivan and Company in Pueblo, Sargeant Malo and Company in Denver, Boettcher and Company in Denver and Harris Upham and Company in Denver. It would also appear that he closely followed the advice given by these professionals. He kept careful and detailed handwritten entries of these investments.

He recorded each company by name, the number of shares owned, the value and the dividends received. The total values of the stocks and bonds were recorded on January 1 and July 1 of each year. Dividends and interest were recorded quarterly. He followed this practice for his own assets until shortly before his death in December 1975.

The available journals kept by Frank Sr. show—after the five years of the Great Depression, on January 1, 1936—total assets of $124,211.90: $95,889.00 in stocks, $26,073.00 in bonds, and cash of $2,249.90. By January 1, 1937, the portfolio value had grown to $146,416; then, by January 1, 1938, it had dropped to $113,463.00, and at January 1, 1939, it had returned to $134,162.00. The author makes the assumption that the drop in value was related to the stock market decline in 1938, to funds used to build Frank's home at 1302 Gunnison and to funds used to purchase land and build the new store at Fourth and Rood.[108]

COLORADO'S MOST MODERN MARKET (1939)

When the Prinster brothers opened Grand Junction's first supermarket in 1939, supermarkets were a rare phenomenon in the United States. Of the few that did exist, most were warehouse-type stores where customers picked their groceries out of open boxes.

Piggly Wiggly was the unusual exception. The first Piggly Wiggly was opened in Memphis, Tennessee, on September 9, 1916, by Clarence Saunders, who patented the concept of self-service. Customers entered the revolutionary store through turnstiles and walked through a maze of shelves containing groceries from which they selected their goods, placed them in their hand-carried baskets and continued on to a cashier.

The Piggly Wiggly phenomenon grew rapidly, and by the end of the 1930s, there were more than twenty-six thousand Piggly Wiggly stores in the United States. By the time the Prinster brothers opened their City Market at Fourth and Rood, Grand Junction's Piggly Wiggly had been bought out by the Safeway chain. However, Grand Junction's Safeway store couldn't hold a candle to the new store created by the Prinster brothers.

City Market opened with great fanfare, garnering the top headline on the front page of the October 11, 1939 *Daily Sentinel*: "City Market Has Formal Opening on Thursday," with the subhead, "Widely Known Grocery Firm at Home in a New Beautiful Edifice." This was followed by a full front page of information on City Market and the Prinster brothers.[109]

In September 1939, not only the biggest grocery store on the Western Slope but also, for a time, the largest supermarket in all of Colorado opened its doors to much acclaim. *Author's collection.*

Seven months after the grand opening, the *Grocer's Digest*, a national trade magazine published in Chicago, featured a photo of the interior of City Market on its cover and touted it in a major article ("City Market—A Tribute to Independent Enterprises"). The article proclaimed that City Market was the most modern market in Colorado and the Rocky Mountains.[110]

After describing the Brothers Four and their history, the story gave details about the store's modern exterior and state-of-the-art interior:

> *The outside of the $75,000 store is built entirely of brick and tile, the walls being faced with pink brick. Horizontal bands of green glazed structural tile and heavy glass blocks complete the modern and attractive setting. Over the main show window a red neon sign on a green background proudly displays the name "City Market" to all who pass by. To accommodate the many automobiles belonging to customers, a large parking lot was especially constructed.*
>
> *As you enter this impressive structure you are struck with a feeling of well-planned immensity. Everything in the way of fixtures reflects the very latest style and design, giving you the impression—a well-founded*

impression—that convenience in shopping and an attractive, inviting appearance have been key notes of the design of this store.

Just inside the entrance, on the right side, there is a handsome, dark green leather upholstered lounge for use of those customers who might be waiting for a companion to complete their shopping. Here, too, are a number of "basket carts" for the use of customers as they pass through the wide aisles buying the groceries they need.

Walking down the first of the three wide aisles, you are aware of massive displays of canned goods and items such as tea and coffee...sections and sections of them. Then come the meat and dairy departments, finished in spotless, sanitary white porcelain. Behind the attractive array of meats and dairy products is a section called the service department. Here, unseen by public eyes, is located a packaging room, a vegetable cleaning room, a refrigerated cooler for vegetables, a large receiving room, men's and women's washrooms, and even a freight elevator which services the main floor and the basement in which several carloads of merchandise is stored.

Leaving the service department and looking toward the front of the store, the customer sees another impressive array of merchandise, principally packaged and carton goods such as cereal, soaps, etc. At the extreme front of the store, just inside the two check-out counters are the colorful fresh produce and bakery departments, two of the most popular spots in the entire store.

Leaving City Market you can not help realizing its entire atmosphere is one of beauty and friendliness—a friendliness upon which the Prinster Brothers have built up an enterprising business.[111]

The Denver architects, Atchison and Emery, said they did considerable study of outstanding grocery markets in Denver, New York, Boston and Hartford, Connecticut, to provide the latest methods of merchandising.

Perhaps most astonishing of all were the brothers themselves. Who would believe they paid cash not only for the land on which their new store was situated but for the construction as well—and during the heart of the Depression? Add to this the fact that Paul, Frank and Leo never had more than a sixth-grade education. This amazing new City Market was a testament not only to the hard work of the Brothers Four but also to their astute business practices. Putting profits back into improvements, paying cash instead of borrowing and focusing on customer satisfaction at all costs were just a few examples of their business acumen. By involving themselves in service organizations and generously contributing to community fundraisers, the brothers also had established themselves among Grand Junction's top business leaders in 1939.

"We have never doubted that the growth of Western Colorado would be continuous and steady," Frank was quoted as saying. "The new modern and beautiful buildings going up all over the community convinced us that we were right in our estimate of the place we chose to spend our lives."

Backstory Notes

At the time of the opening of City Market, the design included a parking lot for, at most, fifty cars. By today's standards, the lot was very small, but for its time, it provided an attractive amenity. When it opened, the parking lot was a featured element. The *Daily Sentinel* special edition of Wednesday evening, October 11, 1939, noted, "Ample Parking. Recognition of the constant parking problem confronting the average shopper was made by placing the building 50 feet back from Rood Avenue to provide ample parking space for City Market patrons. This parking area is paved with concrete, and parking stalls have been indicated by painted lines and expansion joints on the pavement."

However, the new store's location at Fourth and Rood was a high-traffic intersection. The Federal Building was directly across the street to the north, Safeway to the west and the post office at the northwest corner. For a time, there also was a bowling alley immediately east of the store.

City Market's parking lot quickly became inadequate, congested and the scene of confusion, fender benders and a lot of complaints. Frank Jr. was the store manager from the late 1940s until the store closed in 1956. He had to deal with it. His wife, Josephine R. (Roessler) Prinster, a frequent shopper at the store, became very frustrated with the parking lot problem. Never shy about expressing her opinion, Josephine often did so by writing letters to the editor at the *Daily Sentinel*.

One evening after working long hours, Frank Jr. came home and, as was his habit, sat down to read the evening paper while waiting for dinner. On the editorial page, he saw a letter complaining vehemently about the parking lot congestion at City Market. It listed the perils, problems and hardships for shoppers with small children and large bags of groceries. It then admonished, "The short-sighted management had better wake up and do something about it."

The letter was signed Josephine Prinster. Frank was not happy.

THE EXPANSION YEARS (1940–1956)

The new store at Fourth and Rood, completed in October 1939, was successful beyond the brothers' dreams. Sales and profits for one day in the new store amounted to more than the old store had reached in a month. The Prinster brothers had survived the Depression without debt. They lived in nice homes, drove new cars, were content in their family lives and enjoyed respect within the community.

For now, Safeway posed their only challenge. The two stores were right across from each other on Fourth Street. Soon after the new City Market store opened, Safeway launched an aggressive campaign to undercut the brothers by lowering its prices, and the "banner wars" began.

Safeway would post its sale prices on attention-getting banners in its storefront windows, and then City Market would post a banner with an even lower price for the same product…and perhaps include an additional item. It was almost laughable the way these two competing grocery stores went back and forth until they were offering prices so low that the product was almost free. Ice cream, for instance, went down to five cents per quart and ground beef to five cents per pound. Of course, customers were ecstatic. City Market occupied the Fourth and Rood store until the Prinsters built a new store at Fourth and Grand in 1956, but the price wars continued into the 1960s through full-page ads in the *Daily Sentinel*.

On December 7, 1941, Japan attacked Pearl Harbor. The United States entered World War II. For the first time since the Great Depression, the brothers had a serious new challenge to face: rationing. The federal government needed to control supply and demand in order to maintain levels of provisions for the troops abroad and also to prevent hoarding. Posters from the Office of War stated simply, "Do with less so they will have more," and, "Be patriotic; sign your country's pledge to save the food."

Each family member was issued a rationing book that regulated the amount of commodities they could obtain, from gasoline to shoes to severe limits on certain food items. People coped by planting neighborhood "victory gardens" and learning to can foods in order to supplement their rations. Meat was a rare item on the family menu because it required too many coupons. Consumers substituted eggs and cottage cheese for steak and hamburger. At the grocery checkout stand, customers had to present their coupons for the rationed items they purchased. Rather than being counted individually, the coupons were bundled and weighed. The total weight of the bundles was submitted to the proper authorities for accounting.

The responsibility of collecting redeemed ration coupons fell to the carry-out clerks. Things could become hectic when crowds of shoppers were checking out, and the carry-out clerks sometimes forgot to collect the coupons. Of course, this delighted the customers.[112]

Most grocery stores throughout the country were hit hard financially by rationing. City Market was also affected but survived better than most. This was due in large measure to the state-of-the-art design of the new store. Directly behind the retail meat counter on the main sales floor was a refrigerated room for cutting meat. Dressed lambs, halves of pork and front and hind quarters of beef could be brought into this space for processing on overhead tracks directly from the trucks delivering them to the back doors of the store or up an elevator from the meat cooler in the basement. The basement had a refrigerated cooler for storing the meat products, as well as the fish and poultry inventory. The basement also contained a complete smokehouse with a sophisticated exhaust system for smoking meats, large grinders for making hamburger and sausage and big vats for rendering lard. The brothers were able to produce everything they needed for the meat counter upstairs: sausage, bacon, hams, ground products and all cuts of beef, lamb and pork. This ability to process meat products within the store became critical to the store's operation during the difficult rationing years of World War II.

Frank Sr.'s son Joe remembered how this processing center in the basement got them through the war years:

> *The government controlled the packing houses, which could only supply what the government allowed. As City Market had its own processing center, we could get livestock from local ranchers and turn them into consumer salable items. The livestock was slaughtered at a local slaughter plant, then the dressed carcasses and quarters of beef were delivered to the City Market store.*
>
> *We seemed to be unique in this area, as we had people coming to us from the big cities telling us we had the best selection and best quantities in the country. We had government inspectors, the ones responsible for enforcing the ration quotas, visiting us all the time. We never got fined. Their wives sent most of the inspectors to us, as they could get stuff from us that wasn't available anywhere else. Funny thing was that, as word spread, we had other government officials from other regions come to visit us, and they always bought something. They would tell us that no company in the big cities was offering the meat selection we were.*

> *During the early days of the war, I was working in the basement of the meat shop. Paul would have me grind huge vats of hamburger for one customer. When I asked who the customer was and why so much meat, he would tell me it was either for the Italian POW camp in Fruita or the German POW camp in Grand Junction. We weren't too happy about feeding the enemy, but the money was important to keeping the business going.*[113]

The war years also had other challenges and tolls exacted when the sons of the brothers were called to serve. Paul's son, Paul Jr., was called to the U.S. Army and served in France. Frank's son Joe went to war in 1944. He saw action in the Battle of the Bulge and returned a decorated veteran, one of only eleven survivors in his platoon. After World War II, Frank Sr.'s son Clarence (Brother Nicholas) served in the U.S. Navy, and his youngest son, Teo, served in the U.S. Marine Corps. Leo's adopted son, Andrew, served in the U.S. Navy, and Jack, Paul's son, served in the U.S. Air Force.

Despite the war, the brothers continued to put capital back into their business and did not veer from their fundamental philosophy of investing in the latest equipment, maintaining a super-clean store, extending no credit and selling meats and groceries cheaper than anyone else. By war's end, their company was firmly established, and their business philosophy had paid off.

Paul and Frank were now in their mid-fifties and had devoted nearly four decades to the grocery and meat business. Paul's son Jack observed that he thought Paul and Frank would have been content with one store that would support them and their families. Beyond that, they would have been fine just spending time tending their gardens and going for long Sunday drives. They were at a comfortable place in their lives and did not need any more long days and grueling work hours. But Leo was different. By now, he was clearly the boss, always the pusher, always the Kingfish and always ambitious. Sunday drives and flower gardens were not his style. Leo had something else: a vision.

Like most captains of industry, Leo had a goal in mind. He remembered how their father, Joseph, expanded his own stores from La Junta to Lamar, then to Swink and Rocky Ford, all with varying degrees of success. Although Leo's ambitions as a teenager may not have been in the grocery business, he had been a keen observer and student of how a business should be run.

Leo's vision was simple, valid and based on sound reasoning. He saw growth potential in the small towns across the Western Slope. As he explained it to his brothers, each of these towns was ripe for a grocery store, but not more than two in each town. It was critical that they become the first store in the market.

Leo first took his idea to Frank, who had always been Leo's confidant and sounding board. Leo would not do anything unless Frank agreed or approved. He knew if he could persuade Frank that Paul and Clarence would follow. Leo convinced Frank and his brothers to build a chain of City Markets in the growing small towns in the region.

The expansion years began while the war was still on. Leo had the good fortune to meet Cliff Baldridge, a man who became instrumental in helping him implement his vision, especially in the southern part of western Colorado. Short, slightly built, soft-spoken and a confirmed teetotaler, Cliff was the antithesis of Leo in personality. Nevertheless, they worked well together.

Born in Plateau City near Collbran in 1908, Cliff had served as a flight instructor for the U.S. Army Air Corps in Grand Junction in the first few

Joe C. Prinster, apprentice butcher, circa 1943. *Courtesy of Dan Prinster and the Joseph C. Prinster family.*

years of the war. He worked for the Piggly Wiggly store, and then in 1938, he became the manager of a combination food and appliance store in Fruita. In 1944, he met Leo and joined the City Market organization with just a handshake to seal the deal.[114]

In early 1944, an opportunity presented itself in Montrose, and it is believed that Cliff brought it to Leo's attention. The Safeway store in Montrose had burned down, resulting in the business defaulting on its lease, thus making the location available. During wartime, it was not easy to build new structures because of material rationing, particularly for private industry. But under the regulations of the day, a property that had burned could be replaced. The Prinsters bought the land and built their second new store.

On a handshake, Leo not only made Cliff manager of the Montrose store but also a partner in it. Cliff eventually joined the company's executive management team.

While he was the Montrose store manager, Cliff became an influential member of the community. As an executive in the City Market organization, he was particularly helpful with the expansion efforts into Cortez, Alamosa, Durango and other towns and cities in the southern part of the market. He

Cliff Baldridge. *Author's collection.*

The Prinster brothers opened their first Montrose City Market store in 1944. *Courtesy of Mike Keenan.*

was detail-oriented and disciplined and ran his store by rules and policies so clearly communicated that everyone knew what was expected of them. Although quiet in personality and demeanor, he maintained an air of authority about him.

Leo relied on Cliff to be his eyes and ears to help the expansion effort. Although they were complementary and worked well together, there was one notable conflict between Cliff and Leo. In the early 1950s, after the Durango store was opened and running, the next expansion target was Cortez. Leo sent Cliff to look for a location there, and Cliff found a prospect in the center of the town near the courthouse. Cliff entered into a purchase option and paid for the option with his own money. He then made the trip to Grand Junction and met with Leo at his home. Leo looked at the information on the location, thought about it and reacted in a way that surprised Cliff. Leo complained that the site would not do, the price was too high and there was too much land; it was therefore not acceptable. Furthermore, Leo refused to reimburse Cliff for the option payment.

After Leo finished ranting, Cliff called Leo's bluff. Cliff stood up and informed Leo that he'd had enough and would quit. As he walked toward the door, Leo quickly relented, called Cliff back and agreed to pay the option money, and by 1956, City Market no. 8 was built in Cortez.

Shortly before he died in 1995, Cliff Baldridge was inducted into the Colorado Business Hall of Fame along with the likes of Adolph Coors, Claude Boettcher and Charles Gates.

The Montrose City Market opened in 1944, and the Delta store opened one year later. This happened in response to a request from a young man named Dick Tally who had a small independent store there. He approached Leo about backing him in a new store venture. Leo ultimately agreed and made Dick a partner in the Delta City Market that opened in October 1945. Three years later, the brothers took another gamble and opened their fourth store in the little mining, ranching and tourist town of Glenwood Springs. By 1948, City Market owned a chain of four stores. This increase in volume quickly cramped their ability to supply their stores properly. That same year, they acquired property at First Street and Colorado Avenue in Grand Junction that had rail access, and they built a warehouse. It was designated the Colorado Warehouse Grocers Inc. The warehouse was quite small, seventy-five by one hundred feet, but it was the first step toward meeting the increased business and volume demands of the new stores. The warehouse was never a static operation. Over the years, it grew like a Lego creation to meet the constantly growing sales volume.

The warehouse needed more than the railroad to deliver to its outlying stores in Montrose, Delta and Glenwood Springs. The solution came with a local independent trucker named Dewey Miracle. Dewey's semi-tractor had dual exhaust pipes running up each side of the tractor cab, and he kept those pipes polished to a spit-and-shine standard. One could see the pipes flash in the sunlight when he pulled up to a store for delivery. The tractors were all painted yellow with black trim, and these colors became City Market's signature for many years. Leo had conferred with the Colorado State Highway Patrol and learned that yellow was the easiest color to see and therefore the safest to use for highway vehicles. Leo arranged for City Market to buy the trucks for Dewey, who paid the company back by delivery services and eventually owned the trucks outright.[115]

City Market now had a trucking fleet of one tractor and a couple of trailers. The brothers were ready for the next wave of expansion.

Acquiring inventory for resale was always a major challenge. Meat products and produce in season could be bought locally, but groceries and general merchandise were more difficult to purchase at competitive pricing. Their primary source for these products was the C.S. Morey Mercantile Company in Denver. Established by C.S. Morey in 1884, the business manufactured, packaged and marketed all kinds of food products, as well as

The burgeoning fleet of City Market trucks and tractors was highly visible in those yellow and black colors, circa 1955. *Author's collection.*

everything from brooms to chewing tobacco. It had grown into an empire, becoming the largest wholesaler in the Rocky Mountains until its sale to Continental Foods in 1956.[116]

City Market wanted to lower its costs and devised a plan to circumvent its wholesale suppliers. The brothers would buy directly from the producers. One example was a large purchase of sugar. They planned a big promotional sale and had a railroad car go directly to Holly Sugar to pick up the order. This proved to be very successful and started a pattern going forward for other direct purchases. The next step was to start their own wholesale operation. City Market leased a multistory building on South Fifth Street, a location that later became Litton Warehouse. In 1949, the brothers built the Colorado Wholesale Grocers Inc.

The warehouse was heated by a coal furnace, and the coal bin was located on the east side of the building, right next to the buying and accounting offices. There was no air conditioning, so in the summer, the windows had to be opened. In those days, the trains were all steam-driven and coal-fired. Soot from the engines was constantly coming in through the windows, settling in the files, coating papers and the office furniture. The warehouse operation was small and crude, but it was an important step toward meeting the increased business and volume demands of the new stores.[117]

Dewey Miracle took such pride in his rig that it was always clean and intensely polished. *Author's collection.*

The trucks allowed City Market to supply the growing chain of stores efficiently without dependence on rail service. *Author's collection.*

In August 1950, the second Grand Junction City Market opened for business at Ninth Street and North Avenue. It was a ten-thousand-square-foot modern contemporary creation of masonry, glass and steel, with open ceilings that exposed steel trusses, providing a lighter, more airy interior. It was a very innovative design for the region. The interior color scheme consisted of pastel tones of gray, buff, rust and green. It opened to great fanfare, and Clarence was installed as manager. Leo Oleskevich, an up-and-coming management candidate, was appointed Clarence's assistant manager, but not for long. He and several others were moved down to Durango to open and run City Market no. 6.[118]

By now, the Prinster sons had returned from military service and were ready and impatient to take their places in their fathers' growing enterprise. Frank Jr., who had not gone into the military service, had been actively working since 1939 and had assumed a growing load of management duties. Now his two brothers and two cousins were ready to take on some of that responsibility.

The Prinsters were always on the lookout for merchandising partnerships. *Left to right*: Paul Jr., Frank Sr. and Frank Jr. *Author's collection.*

Paul Jr. went to work in the meat department with his father, while his cousin Joe took over supervising the meat operations. Joe's brother Teo, recently home from the Marine Corps, also went to work in management, and when they returned, Leo's son Andrew and Paul's son Jack began working in the family business. The family team was now complete and in place.

Then came the uranium boom. The "U-boom" of the 1950s presented tremendous opportunities and more challenges for the four brothers and their sons. Thousands of uranium miners—many with no more than battery-powered Geiger counters and shovels—scoured the adobe hills and arid canyons of western Colorado and eastern Utah looking for the mother lode of U238. This was no economic "boomlet"; it was an atomic boom. An article in *Life* magazine predicted that Grand Junction would become the largest city west of the Mississippi.

Uranium fever was inflamed by the Cold War. The federal government actively recruited miners from all over the country by offering bonuses and guaranteed prices. One could even purchase a forty-five-cent how-to pamphlet called *Prospecting for Uranium*, composed by the Atomic Energy Commission. A reliable domestic source of uranium was needed by the Defense Department to fuel the chain reaction in atomic weapons. On the Colorado Plateau—which included not only parts of Colorado but also

Utah, Arizona and New Mexico—lay the largest deposit of uranium in the world. It soon became the site of 550 uranium mines, 500 of them located in Colorado and Utah.[119]

In those vast, unpopulated wild lands, there were no stores of any kind. Some of the wealthier uranium miners used airplanes to prospect; then, once a week, they would fly their wives to Grand Junction to shop at the supermarket. The grocery business was enjoying increased profits from all the activity, so the Prinster family decided to expand even more to meet the demand.

For the first time, however, the capital demands of expansion required them to deviate from their pay-as-you-go philosophy. They had to borrow from banks and other lenders. Building the warehouse, expanding into Durango and opening their second large store in Grand Junction put a tremendous strain on their capital. Nevertheless, the loans were paid back quickly.

Then a second energy trend began to sprout in 1950: oil shale. In an attempt to stay ahead of the curve, the brothers opened City Market no. 7 in Rifle. The next big step came with City Market no. 8 in Cortez in 1955.

Frank Jr. attended a merchandising convention in Chicago and returned home with more than a few good ideas, circa 1950. *Author's collection.*

According to Laurena Maynes Davis, who wrote for the company newsletter *Express Lines*, "The opening of an eighth store—this one in Cortez—was too much for the Front Range to ignore."

The *Denver Post* on December 14, 1955, featured the Prinsters in a banner headline on page one: "Meet the Prinsters: Builders of the Western Slope Grocery Empire." The article noted that in thirty-two years, the Prinsters had become major figures in Colorado merchandising. Their City Market enterprise was worth $2 million. They employed 150 persons and easily ranked as one of western Colorado's largest independent businesses.[120]

The *Denver Post* reporter asked Leo many questions about store personnel and family members. When the reporter asked if there were any problems with disagreements among family members, Leo said, "We have little squabbles now and then, of course. But arguments are time-consuming, and we're far too busy selling groceries to indulge ourselves. We are hard on the young people [meaning family members in the business], but they take it well and work right along with us."[121] This was an interesting

The City Market store in Cortez opened in 1956. *Author's collection.*

The Brothers Four at the groundbreaking in March 1956 at Fourth and Grand Avenue, the location built to replace the store that was built in 1939. *Left to right*: Frank, Paul, Leo and Clarence. *Author's collection.*

City Market at Fourth and Grand Avenue, August 1956. *Left to right*: Andrew, Paul J., Joe, Clarence, Teo, Jack, Frank Jr., Leo and Frank Sr. *Author's collection.*

statement in light of what was to come. Leo was both a visionary and a hard-nosed businessman, but as future events would show, he had a limited understanding of how explosive this "family squabbling" would turn out to be.

Shortly after the completion of the City Market at Fourth and Grand in 1956, the oldest brother and City Market founder, Paul, died. His death in August of that year would mark a major shift within the Prinster family dynamics.

Backstory Notes

About the time the Montrose City Market opened (in December 1944), the brothers made an attempt to start another store in Montrose. This store was opened under the name of Pay-Less. A Montrose newspaper article (year unknown) reported:

> *Opening Friday, December 8, the city of Montrose has a new supermarket, the Pay-Less, installed by the Prinster brothers, Leo, Frank, Paul, and Clarence, Frank Prinster Jr., and Paul Prinster, who is now in service in France. Associated in the ownership and in active charge of the management is Clifford Baldridge, who has been for some time associated with City Market. The securing of even larger buying volume was the objective of the Prinster brothers in opening the new Montrose market, as increased buying will make possible sales at lower prices. Already City Market is known throughout the country as the large volume store with a sales capacity that enables the management to take advantage of opportunities of buying which in turn are reflected on to the customer. The Prinster brothers operate a wholesaling department in connection with the Montrose store.*

From the article, it appears that the brothers were operating two stores in Montrose, the City Market and the Pay-Less. There is no information given or found as to the fate of the Pay-Less venture. From the article, it appears that the store was planned to operate as what is known today as a warehouse store and sell to ranchers and miners at reduced service, higher volume, or bulk at a lower cost.[122]

Succession and the Corporate World (1949–1956)

In 1939, when Paul, Leo and Frank purchased the site for the new store on Fourth and Rood, the land was conveyed to them as "Joint Tenants with Right of Survivorship."[123] The share each of them owned was not specified, and a joint tenant arrangement meant that if any one of the brothers died, the surviving brothers would inherit the deceased brother's ownership share. A few years after the store opened in the fall of 1939, Jim Groves, the company attorney, advised the brothers of problems with that decision. He told them that if something happened to one of them, that brother's family would have no legal rights to the business. He recommended that they make partnership agreements that would define their ownership amounts and make sure their families were protected.

Paul, Frank and Leo agreed that their ownership was one-third each, but they also agreed that the younger generation should be encouraged to enter the family enterprise. They divided the business into eighteen shares, six shares for each. Paul Sr. then gave one of his shares to his son Paul, Frank Sr. gave one of his shares to his son Frank Jr. and Leo gave two of his shares to his younger brother, Clarence. The four brothers and two sons became co-partners and operated d.b.a. ("doing business as") City Market. The ownership of these shares would play a pivotal role in the future of the City Market enterprise.

The City Market enterprise grew into a collection of corporations and partnerships. Each entity had a specific function and purpose. They were interrelated but not bound by any formal agreement. In December 1954, four corporations were established to own and operate all the activities that had been doing business as "City Market."[124] Colorado Wholesale Grocers Inc. was created to own and operate the warehouse and trucking business. Prinster Brothers Inc. was formed to be the real estate company and was the largest corporation in terms of assets. North Avenue City Market Inc. was formed to operate the store at Ninth Street and North Avenue, which had been built in 1950. City Market Inc. was created to operate the new Grand Avenue store that replaced the original store at Fourth and Rood. The percentage of ownership of the stock in these newly formed corporations mirrored the ownership that had been established by the brothers and their sons when they opened the Fourth and Rood store in 1939. The shareholders and directors in each corporation were identical. The board of directors consisted of Frank Sr., Frank Jr., Leo, Clarence and Paul Jr. Paul Sr. was not interested in sitting on the board or being an officer but was content just being a shareholder. Leo was the president of all the corporations.

The other group of entities that made up the City Market enterprise was the partnerships. These were formed with the brothers, their sons and various individuals who were employees associated with the business but who were not family members. The owners and the percentage owned were not the same in each partnership, but the partnerships all operated under the umbrella of City Market.

These partnerships owned the City Markets in Montrose, Delta, Durango, Cortez and Glenwood Springs. By 1955, City Market consisted of four corporations—City Market Inc., Colorado Wholesale Grocers Inc., Prinster Brothers Inc. and North Avenue City Market Inc.—and five partnerships that owned the City Market stores in Cortez, Glenwood Springs, Durango, Delta and Montrose.[125]

The rapid expansions over the ten-year period from the 1940s to the early 1950s were financed with the internal cash flow and profits generated by the business. Leo was focused on expansion throughout the Western Slope, and he was determined to do it without bank debt. Attorney Jim Groves and accountant Walt Dalby helped him devise ways to finance the expansion without borrowing from banks. The plan had three primary objectives: control of the corporations would remain in Leo's hands, all profits would be retained in the corporations for use as Leo wanted and taxes would be minimized. This was accomplished by having multiple corporations. In the 1950s, income taxes on corporations were low on the first $25,000, but after that, they escalated to 50 percent. Thus, there was a benefit to having multiple corporations and rents adjustable as needed for tax purposes. This was a common practice and smart management. Congress did not wise up until the 1970s.[126]

Although the corporations would generate cash sufficient to finance expansion, cash available for dividends or bonuses would be curtailed. In lieu of payouts to management and shareholders for bonuses or dividends, each corporation issued debentures. The debentures were for a ten-year duration, with an interest rate of 4.5 percent. The interest was to be paid annually. They were issued in 1955 and were payable at maturity in 1965. The total amount of the issued debentures was $530,000 ($4,500,000 in today's dollars).[127] The corporations kept the cash and profits for expansion. Leo controlled the corporations. In the words of Curt Robinson, the company accountant, "Leo ruled with an iron hand."[128]

In August 1956, City Market no. 1 at Fourth and Rood was closed and replaced by a brand-new, state-of-the-art store at Fourth Street and Grand Avenue. Two weeks after it opened, Paul Sr. died after a long illness. What followed was a tumultuous year for the entire family. Father Eddie died in December of that year, and Jody, Frank Sr.'s wife of forty-two years, died the following February.

Paul (together with wife Goldie, sons Paul and Jack and daughter Barbara Jane) owned 33.3 percent of the collection of corporations that made up City Market. They also held 33.3 percent of the debentures that had been issued to shareholders in 1955.

Concerned that his mother would not have sufficient funds for her support, twenty-six-year-old Jack felt that it was imperative to settle his father's estate as soon as possible. He hoped to sell the estate's interests back to the company or to other family members. Initially, he enlisted the help of his brother-in-law, attorney Bill Raso. Bill was primarily a real estate lawyer, and he advised Jack to get an experienced estate attorney. Bill recommended T. Raber Taylor, a well-known, highly regarded Denver attorney who was a Harvard Law graduate.[129]

A series of meetings ensued. Jack, his attorney Taylor, Leo, Walt Dalby (City Market's accountant) and Jim Groves, the company's (and Leo's) personal attorney, entered into negotiations to establish a sale price for their interest in the four corporations. Things did not go well. Jack felt that Dalby and Groves were only on Leo's side and were not willing to do anything in his interest or that of his mother, sister or the estate.

Growing increasingly frustrated, Jack issued a veiled threat at one of these meetings. He told Dalby, Groves and Leo that during the time he had worked in the buying and bookkeeping departments, he had learned of information about some financial irregularities. Jack did not, in fact, have any such information. He was just trying to gain some negotiating leverage to increase the price of the stock. Instead, he only angered Groves and Leo, and the negotiations soon ended.

On the advice of his attorney, Jack decided to sell the estate's interest to an outside party. Taylor put him in contact with Lloyd King of King Soopers in Denver. King made a trip to Grand Junction and looked into the business and its properties. Leo personally escorted King around and was very cordial to him, but King had no interest in buying a minority share in the company. This first meeting between Leo and Lloyd King had unforeseen but far-reaching consequences.

Incensed at the intimidation and feeling threatened that Jack would try to bring an outsider into the business, Leo called a meeting of the board. Leo is quoted by his daughter Penny as saying, "The family is as solid as a stump of wood, and no one from the outside will be allowed to come in." Even though Jack was a stockholder and the corporate secretary, as well as an employee, the board agreed to fire him. Teo, Jack's first cousin, was given the task of telling Jack that he was terminated.

Both Teo and Jack worked at the North Avenue City Market. The next morning, Teo asked Jack for his key, using the excuse that he had lost his and needed to make another copy. At the end of the day, when Jack asked for his key back, Teo told him about the board meeting and that he had been terminated.[130]

Jack was furious. He decided to leave Grand Junction permanently and return to college. He enrolled in Georgetown University with the goal to enter the diplomatic service but soon concluded that it was not the right course for him. He moved to Southern California and enrolled at the University of Southern California to study business. While there, he worked as a grocery buyer for Market Wholesale Grocery and rose to the position of vice-president. He finished his business education and obtained his degree from Woodbury University. Through the help of an old business acquaintance of his father's, he obtained a position with the Safeway Corporation. Over the course of his career, he rose to the position of senior vice-president and corporate director of marketing for the Safeway Corporation. He retired from Safeway in 1985.

Backstory Notes

Between 1939 and 1956, Paul, Frank and Leo each made gifts of their shares to their children. Leo, after giving two shares to his brother Clarence, later gave shares outright and in trust to his daughter Patricia and his son Andrew. Paul gave a share to his son Paul Jr.

When Frank's son Joe returned from the war, Frank gave one of his five shares to him. Over the next decade, Frank divided his remaining four shares among his other children. At the time of Paul's death in 1956, Paul and his immediate family owned one-third of the corporations. Frank owned only a small interest in North Avenue City Market Inc., and his children collectively owned the balance of his original one-third interest. Leo held 11.11 percent and—together with 11.11 percent gifted to his children and 11.11 percent owned by his brother Clarence—Leo effectively controlled one-third. This shareholder information is taken from and based on the debenture list dated September 1967.

THE TAKEOVER (1957–1963)

Paul's estate was closed in May 1957, and his ownership in the four corporations passed to Goldie, Jack and Barbara Jane.[131] But their minority interest, in a privately held corporation, was essentially unsalable. They were locked in. Leo, Frank and Clarence made no effort to purchase the heirs' interest despite its significant value.

Curt Robinson, who handled the City Market account for the Dalby firm, speculates that the reason for the inaction was the cost of expansion and the need for cash for that purpose. Leo controlled the company and its money, so he could proceed with business as usual without having to purchase Paul's interest.[132] This lack of action would come back to haunt Leo.

Large regional and national firms were beginning to notice City Market in western Colorado. It was in 1957 that the Dillon Companies, a supermarket chain headquartered in Hutchinson, Kansas, purchased the King Soopers stores in Denver. At that time, King Soopers was a chain of nine stores started by Lloyd King in Arvada, Colorado. Shortly after Dillon acquired King Soopers, the chain came knocking on City Market's door. It is believed that Lloyd King, as a result of his trip to Grand Junction at Jack's request, made Dillon Companies aware of City Market as a possible acquisition. The brothers met with Dillon representatives but were not interested. A few years after that, the Albertsons chain approached City Market. Albertsons officials said that if the company couldn't acquire City Market, it would come into the Grand Junction market and compete with them head-to-head.

Frank Jr., Joe and Teo traveled to the Albertsons headquarters in Boise, Idaho, to talk with corporate executives. Albertsons did make an offer to buy, but it was a lowball offer, and no agreement was reached. One result of that meeting, however, was that it made the City Market management aware of the problems presented by their fractured organizational structure. The younger men could easily see that the company needed to be updated and streamlined to be more competitive and made attractive as a sale prospect.[133]

Starting in 1962, the younger generation embarked on efforts to streamline and reorganize the company. Their endeavors were aided by accountant Curt Robinson and attorney Jim Groves—with, of course, the blessing of Leo.

The first step was to create a management group to run and direct all of the stores. This management group was designated Group A. Its seven members included Frank Jr., Joe, Teo, Paul Jr., Gene Haggerty, Hale Luff and Leo's son Andrew.[134] The decision mechanism was that a vote of four of the seven members could make a binding decision. Curt Robinson believes that Group A was formed on a handshake and that its hidden agenda was to curtail Leo's dictatorship and control.

Group A oversaw the management of all the retail stores and warehousing owned by the four different City Market corporations and the operation of the retail stores owned by the partnerships. Consolidating all the real estate and buildings not owned by the corporations into limited partnerships was high on Group A's agenda. These partnerships took over ownership of the Montrose, Delta, Durango, Cortez and Glenwood Springs stores. In essence, Group A now served as general partners of the limited partnerships, and the other owners were the limited partners. This reorganization proceeded gradually and in incremental steps between 1961 and 1967.

As the younger generation took a more active part in the operation of the business, Leo became more difficult. According to Joe, "Instead of encouraging the new blood's endeavors and listening to our ideas, Leo was increasingly abusive and critical, slinging accusations like, 'This time you really did it. You built the store too big; you can't do anything right. I have tried to teach you, and you just don't do it right.'"[135]

We can only imagine why Leo was so critical. Did he think that the younger generation had it too easy, that they were being handed the business on the proverbial silver platter? He couldn't have failed to notice that they were all better educated than he was or that they wouldn't do things the way they had always been done. Or did he sense that his control was being challenged? His grip and influence beginning to slip?

The only one who truly tried to please Leo was Frank Jr., and Leo picked on him the most. Frank Jr.'s younger brother, Joe, recalls an incident that took place one morning in the basement of the new store at Fourth and Grand. Leo confronted Frank when he thought no one was around, but Joe was at the back of the room and witnessed what happened. Leo started to tear into Frank with his "You did not do this or you did not do that right" criticisms. Frank seemed to have had his fill and immediately stopped Leo.

"He really told Leo off," said Joe. "He let him know that he had tried to do everything asked of him, but it was never enough. Frank demanded an apology. Instead of apologizing, Leo said nothing, looked at the ground, then turned and walked off. After that, there was no more criticism directed at Frank."[136]

During the reorganization process, expenditures past and present were audited. It was a very complex ordeal that took a year and a half to complete. In the process, the accountants found invoices for the construction of Leo's swimming pool that had been paid for by the company. Curt took the information to his boss, Walt Dalby, who told him to go talk to the lawyer, Jim Groves. "Groves was the only guy out there Leo would not talk back to," said Curt.

Presented with the invoices, Groves thought for a minute, then looked up and told Curt, "You go talk to Leo. Tell him that if he would like to go to jail, we will just leave those charges right there." Curt dreaded the confrontation. He had witnessed Leo's eruptions on numerous occasions. But instead of blowing up, Leo, to his credit, simply told Curt, "If we can't do it, we can't do it. What do I owe?"[137] This was not the last of Leo's overreaching. It also was discovered that Leo had been charging all the expenses for his annual luxury Hawaiian retreats to the company.

When members of the younger generation learned of this, they were outraged. They recalled how every time Leo (aka "Uncle Son-of-a-Bitch") returned from one of his six-month sojourns to Hawaii, he would call them together in a meeting and instead of saying, "Hello, how's it going?" he would immediately launch into critical attacks on everything they had been doing wrong while he was gone.

When Joe took the information about Leo's expenditures to his father, Frank Sr., Frank didn't see anything wrong with it and defended Leo. Leo had worked hard for the company for years and deserved it. That was Frank's attitude, but this frustrated and irritated Joe.

The younger generation had been fed up with Leo for a long time. This latest revelation was the last straw. Joe, Teo and Gene Haggerty discussed Leo's actions at length and then devised a plan to gain control of the company. Group A controlled the partnerships, and they knew they could get the four controlling votes within Group A. Four of the seven members of Group A could make a binding decision. They calculated that they could get more than 50 percent of the corporations, and thus control, if they could buy the shares owned by Jack, his mother and his sister. At that time, Leo owned or controlled 33 percent of the company. They were sure that Clarence would side with Leo. Paul Jr. was still an unknown.

They contacted Jack in California and opened negotiations to purchase all of his and his mother's and sister's stock in the four corporations. Joe and Teo met with Jack in Salt Lake City to negotiate an agreement. Their offer was $200,000 for the stock. Jack came back and asked for $250,000, which they agreed to. Jack also required that they pay off the outstanding debentures held by himself, his mother and his sister. This would amount to an additional $142,000, plus interest. Jack and his mother and sister agreed to sell.[138]

Their next step was to find the money to pay Jack. They were young workingmen in their mid-thirties with families to support on grocery-store salaries. They did not have $250,000 hidden away under the mattress or in a coffee can. They thought they would have to get a loan, but they also felt that because of Leo's influence in the community, it would have to come from a bank outside of Grand Junction. Otherwise, Leo, who was on his annual retreat in Hawaii at the time, would find out about it.

They did not want their father, Frank Sr., or their brother, Frank Jr., to know what they were up to until they had pulled it all together. Later, Joe said that he did keep his father informed, and although it upset him greatly, he didn't interfere. More importantly, he honored his son's confidence and didn't spill the beans to his brother Leo. Joe said they didn't tell Frank Jr. until after they had made the deal with Jack because they weren't sure if he would side with them or the older guys.

Joe and Teo asked their brother-in-law, Gene Haggerty, to contact a bank in Denver, where Gene's mother had worked. The bank said that it would consider a loan if a local banker in Grand Junction would give them a good character reference. They made an appointment with E.L. Bacon, president of the U.S. Bank in Grand Junction.[139] Bacon was a formidable character. He conducted business at his large desk in the center of the open lobby area of the bank at Fourth and Main. This allowed him to keep an eagle eye on the comings and goings of his employees and customers. An invisible fence existed around E.L.'s desk, and the employees would not approach within ten feet without an approving nod.[140]

Joe and Teo, not knowing for sure what to expect, approached E.L. at his big desk. They explained that they needed a good reference so they could get a loan from a bank in Denver. They told him of their plan and the reason for the loan. E.L. listened to Joe and Teo's request. Finally, he leaned back in his chair, rubbed his nose, looked them over carefully and said, "Why don't I make you the loan?"

After the shock of Bacon's offer sank in, the boys said to Mr. Bacon, "If our Uncle Leo finds out, you will have hell to pay."

E.L. quietly responded, "You boys let me worry about that."[141]

The loan was agreed on with a handshake and the promise that after the boys got control of the company, they would transfer their biggest account from First National Bank to Bacon's bank. "It was the account that had the float," said Curt Robinson. "It also was an unsecured loan at 4 percent. E.L. Bacon knew what was going on and how to make it work," Curt added.

Once they had their loan, they entered into an agreement with Jack on December 16, 1963, and closed the purchase the following January. With their shares and the shares owned by their brothers and sisters included, they could count on votes of more than 50 percent. By then, they had informed their brother Frank Jr., and he added his shares as well. To the surprise of his brothers, Frank Jr. asked to be the one to tell Leo that he was fired.

The following morning, a Saturday, Frank Jr. went to Leo's house with the news. Leo had returned from Hawaii. Frank reported to his brothers afterward that Leo put on "an Academy Award" performance. "He pulled out a big handkerchief and wiped his nose and wiped his mouth and cried, 'Oh those boys. After I spent my life trying to teach them the business, bringing them up in the business, and how to do things, here they are turning on me now that I'm older.' He was still crying when I walked out the door," said Frank.[142]

By Monday morning, Leo was in Jim Groves's office raising hell. The boys found out about this from Bill Hyde, an attorney in Groves's office. Bill said, "Man, your Uncle Leo stomped in here and made all of us get together in Groves' office, and he told us, 'Goddamn you lazy sons of bitches! I want those damn kids to know they can't control this business. I want this shit stopped, and you find a way to do it!' When Leo finally drew a breath, Jim Groves reminded him that he had drawn up the papers for the company and that they were iron-clad. 'There's not a damn thing you can do about it,' he told Leo. 'If they have over 50 percent of the stock, they control the company.'"[143]

Hyde added, "Groves said all of this in a respectful and business-like manner, but when Leo left, I had the impression that Groves was cheering inside."

Afterward, Joe and Teo went to see their father. Frank was living with his daughter Margie by then. They told him what they had done. Frank Sr. didn't say anything. He just stared at them. Frank didn't speak about this again for several years, and neither did Leo. Obviously Leo did his own calculations and realized that the boys had indeed been smart enough to take control. But Leo still had a considerable amount of stock and debentures. Once the boys had control of the company, they realized they were sitting on a lot of money—enough to pay off all the debentures with interest by 1967. And with the help of the proceeds of their own debenture money, they also were able to pay back the bank loan to E.L. Bacon two years later.

Stock ownership was another matter, however. Leo still owned or controlled nearly 33 percent of the company. This would lead to interesting developments a few years later.

Backstory Notes

Gene Haggerty was married to Frank Sr.'s youngest daughter, Lucille Prinster Haggerty. He had come to Grand Junction to attend Mesa College and play baseball for the Mavericks. He later played for the Grand Junction Eagles, a semipro baseball team. Gene and Lucille married, and Gene entered the family business. He became an important part of the warehousing and trucking operations and rose to become vice-president of warehousing.

Hale Luff was originally from California and was stationed in Grand Junction as a member of the U.S. Army Air Corps. While in training as an airman, he met Mary Prinster, one of Frank Sr.'s twin daughters. After the war, they were married, and Hale became an instrumental part of the buying operations for City Market.

Leo's firing was not widely announced or known for some time after the takeover. To the world outside the business, things appeared to continue as usual. On November 23, 1964, the Denver Association of Manufacturers Representatives honored the Prinster family. An article written by Pasquale Marrazzino for the *Rocky Mountain News* stated, in somewhat awkward language:

> *Even in 1923, the Western Slope was remote...The Prinsters began growing and establishing the new stores in the necklace of cities and towns that link Southwestern Colorado. The chain—all owned by the same family, Frank Sr. and Leo Prinster still at the helm, and sons and grandsons fanned out in the area with big supermarket-type stores in Grand Junction Montrose, Durango, Cortez, Rifle, Glenwood Springs,*

> *Delta, and Moab, Utah. It was a visionary taking—a belief in the potential of the Western Slope that has just begun to be realized. And I thought it was nice* [of] *the DAMR—representative sales people of all the big food manufacturers—to bring the whole family to Denver for testimonial. And as a fitting tribute, Walter Garnsey, president of DAMR, presented to Leo Prinster a mural photograph of the La Junta store taken in 1902 that sent the memories stirring.*[144]

James K. Groves enjoyed an illustrious legal career in Colorado and nationally. He was appointed to the Supreme Court of Colorado in 1968 by then governor John A. Love. During his twelve years on the Supreme Court bench, Groves authored more than 540 opinions—many of which are recognized today as landmark decisions.

He was born in Grand Junction in 1910 and after graduating from the University of Colorado Law School, with honors, in 1935, Groves returned to serve his community. From 1940 to 1944, he was Mesa County deputy district attorney. In 1948, he became the Mesa County assistant district attorney, and from 1952 to 1956, he was the Grand Junction city attorney. He formed his own law firm, specialized in water and mineral law and built a reputation as one of the state's best trial attorneys. He founded the nationally recognized Rocky Mountain Mineral Law Foundation and served as its president.

In 1958, he became a member of the House of Delegates of the American Bar Association and eventually was appointed chairman of this arm of the ABA, serving until 1978. He received numerous prestigious awards throughout his career. James K. Groves died in 1980 at the age of seventy.[145]

One of the biggest challenges of this book has been to correctly characterize Uncle Leo. I had occasion to meet and talk with him a few times when I was younger. The experience was always pleasant, not the confrontational and hypercritical experiences remembered by others, especially by my uncles, Joe and Teo. My father, Frank Jr., had his share of unpleasant interchanges with Leo, but he never talked about them. He made sure that all of his children treated Leo with the respect due an elder. When I was engaged to be married, my father insisted that I make an obligatory visit to Leo and introduce him to my fiancée, Sally. Leo was engaging and charming and easily assumed the role of the perfect host and patriarch.

My study of the history and growth of City Market brings me to the conclusion that much of its ultimate success was due to Leo. I agree with Jack Prinster, Leo's nephew, in his observation that most successful organizations have in their history a driver who pushes the whole organization to achieve. Leo filled this role and filled it well. He was indeed the Kingfish. His brothers and employees in the stores gave him this designation.

Without a doubt, he was demanding, manipulative and overly critical. My coauthor Kate Ruland-Thorne, an acute judge of character, compares him to the character J.R. in the TV series *Dallas*. To my mind, he could be Captain Ahab in *Moby-Dick*. He came complete with a thunder-and-lightning persona, a driven vision and a wooden leg.

However, a villain he was not. I think a careful review of events shows that much about Leo belongs on the positive side of the ledger. In addition to his business acumen, he was responsible for generous acts. I believe that he was one of the primary reasons behind the "chit" program that helped the teachers during the Great Depression. He made sure that the business supported the community and charities. After more than ten years of hard work in the little store on North Fourth Street, he gave his younger brother Clarence a substantial part of his ownership. He was genuinely concerned that the business could continue to support the large families who made up the organization.

Leo was autocratic, complex, ambitious, critical, driven and successful. He was always the "Kingfish."

THE MERGER

In 1964, Frank Prinster Jr. replaced Leo as City Market's second president, and a new era began. The Brothers Four were no longer at the helm, but their business philosophy and the principles that had brought their company to its present success remained solidly in place: pay as you go, reinvest in the best equipment, maintain competitive pricing and adhere to customers' needs. These were respected and valued lessons that the younger generation had learned from their forebears.

The younger generation also understood that the new era brought new challenges. Frank Jr. reflected on that period after he and his brothers took control. "Western Colorado was growing, and City Market was constantly looking for new locations," he said. "The new management was affected by the need for a larger warehouse facility. We realized, too, that we needed expertise in the new and different phases that faced the supermarket business.

In addition, we had to deal with the financial requirements of continuing to build our new stores at a rapid pace."[146]

Always on the lookout for new locations, a new way of doing things and new services and products, the Prinsters also searched for capable new talent that would help them meet their goals. One such talented young man was Dick McMillen, who had been a division sales manager for Pacific Fruit Company. Frank Jr. persuaded him to come and work for City Market. Dick would prove to be a great contributor and innovator over the years, and he held the position of executive vice-president upon his retirement in 1993.

When Dick started in 1964, he immediately began to build the produce departments—the major profit centers in the stores. He was instrumental in expanding the warehouse operations to include produce and other perishables so they were not dependent on third-party suppliers. He was also instrumental in developing the bakery and delicatessen departments. He pushed to have a centralized training center, and in the late 1970s, he helped City Market become one of the first stores to incorporate the use of scanners for checkout.[147]

The younger generation continued to make changes in other areas of the business. Frank Jr.'s youngest brother, Teo, took on the real estate side of the business and assumed the responsibility for building and development. Through his efforts, the company acquired an uncanny ability to intuit where to build the next store and to build that store ahead of the competition. It would identify small communities that the national chains had either overlooked or considered too small an area for their operations. After Teo's team identified a new community, the company would build a starter store; find a local, community-minded manager; and then grow with the community. By the time the larger chains returned to take a second look, City Market already had a thriving business in place—a lesson learned from the Brothers Four that worked.

During those first years under new leadership, expansion continued. In 1964, the original Glenwood Springs store was remodeled and expanded. A year later, a new Delta City Market was constructed, and a store was built in Basalt. In 1968, the brothers added a new City Market in Grand Junction at First Street and Orchard Avenue and acquired a store in Rawlins, Wyoming. In 1969, they built a store in Fruita and acquired an existing small store in Aspen; in 1970, they purchased a small store—Bill's Market—in Craig, Colorado.

Dillon Companies in 1965 again approached City Market's management about a possible merger. This time, the younger generation was interested.

They recognized the numerous advantages that a merger could bring to their company.

After Dillon acquired the King Sooper stores in 1957, "Kings" became one of the most successful supermarket chains in the nation. City Market and Dillon had something special in common. Both of their chains reached back into the 1880s, when their founders scratched out their start in small towns. Both had grainy old photos to share showing the sons of their founders posing in front of small cash-and-carry stores. Both had gradually expanded into other communities, and they shared a tradition of supporting their communities and local charities. Dillon Companies Inc. was the larger of the two companies. It became a public company in December 1957 and, twelve years later, was listed on the New York Stock Exchange. These seeds of similarity made for a good match. It would not be a hostile takeover.[148]

The discussions began in 1965 and progressed over several years. Management teams from both companies flew back and forth to each other's headquarters in order to understand how the other approached business. However, completing the deal was no slam-dunk. There was a lot to be done and details to be attended to. Years later, Curt Robinson, reflecting back on those days, commented that the City Market/Dillon merger was one of the most complex transactions of his accounting career.[149]

To begin with, the plan to consolidate the fractionalized nature of the capital structure had to be completed. All the entities that made up the City Market enterprise had to be consolidated into one entity that would qualify for a tax-free exchange. By December 1966, three of the four corporations that made up the enterprise—Colorado Wholesale Grocers Inc., North Avenue City Market Inc. and City Market Inc.—were merged into the newly designated corporation, City Market Inc. Next, all the shareholders had to agree to the merger. At that time, there were forty-five shareholders.[150]

A typical example of a non-family shareholder was Dick Wagaman, the original manager of the Glenwood Springs store. He said, "Leo hired me in the early 1940s to manage the Glenwood Springs store. Leo came there one day to see me. He said, 'Dick, why don't you buy some stock in this store?' I said, 'Leo, I don't have any money.' He said, 'I'll loan you the money, and you pay me back with your dividends.' So that's what I did. After we merged with Dillon, we got a bunch of Dillon stock."

Next, the plan to consolidate the stores owned by the individual partnerships had to be completed. That was accomplished by year's end of 1967. Limited partnerships were created that owned the real estate and the buildings. These limited partnerships then leased the facilities to the

The family, gathered on the occasion of Frank J. Prinster Sr.'s seventy-fifth birthday in 1967. *Back row, left to right*: Andrew Prinster, Rob Peckham, Frank J. Prinster Jr., Paul J. Prinster, Brother Nicholas, Joseph C. Prinster and Leo (Teo) Prinster. *Middle row, left to right*: Gene Haggerty, William Raso, Lucille Haggerty, Inez Prinster, Mary Prinster, Miriam Peckham, Josephine R. Prinster (wife of Frank Jr.), Josephine A. Prinster (wife of Paul J.), Mary Luff, Del Prinster, Marjorie Prinster and Delores Prinster. *Front row, left to right*: Hale Luff, Barbara Jane Raso, Clarence Prinster, Goldie Prinster, Frank J. Prinster Sr., Leo G. Prinster and Bernice Prinster. *Author's collection.*

surviving corporate entity, City Market Inc., for a term of fifteen years. The leases allowed City Market Inc. to control the sites, and they could be transferred to a new owner in a sale or merger.

By 1967, Dillon had made a proposal that was acceptable to the City Market management because it offered many advantages: greater competitive capacity, added capital, increased buying capabilities and access to more modern supermarket-management tools. City Market management recommended the Dillon proposal to the shareholders. They explained that by merging with Dillon, City Market would become a wholly owned subsidiary of Dillon Companies, and Dillon Companies would provide a resource of capital for continued expansion. The current management would remain in place with a commitment from Dillon to a hands-off approach to operations. Joe Prinster said that the Dillon executives assured him that they were not buying bricks and mortar. "We are buying management," they said. It looked to have all the ingredients for a very profitable deal for all parties. Most of the family members and employee shareholders were in favor of the merger and were eager to go through with it.[151]

There was only one obstacle: Leo. He did not like the deal and refused to agree to the merger. He owned a substantial amount of shares in the company and could easily block the transaction. He seemed poised and ready to play the spoiler.

Dillon's president, Ray E. (Ace) Dillon Jr., flew to Grand Junction for the sole purpose of meeting with Leo. Leo asked his accountant, Curt Robinson, to accompany him to this meeting. Curt described what happened:

> *There were only three of us in the room that day: Ace Dillon, Leo and me. The meeting lasted three hours, and I'll never forget it. Ace laid out the terms of the merger, explained what it would mean to each stockholder, what it would do for the company and how everyone would be much better off. He added that the terms of the deal were very favorable to all of the stockholders. When he finished, he waited for Leo to respond, and he did. He said, "No! That's not enough. You're not offering enough money."*
>
> *Ace Dillon's face turned really red. He came as close to exploding as any man I've ever seen in any situation. But he did not blow it. He kept his cool and asked, "How much more do you want?" Ace badly wanted this merger to go through, and he needed Leo's shares or it wouldn't happen. So he and Leo continued to talk.*
>
> *Finally, Ace said, "All right, this is what I'm able to do. If you think the company is worth much more, then let's make a contingent deal. If over the next five years, the company earnings are better than what is projected in our present agreement and the company can hit certain earning targets in excess of our projection, then we will pay an additional 5 percent of the purchase price."*
>
> *That worked, and Ace, Leo and I walked out. At that meeting, the "earn-out" was born. No one in that room—or, for that matter, none of the parties to the merger—could foresee what that earn-out would eventually mean. More than trying to increase the price, I think Leo was just trying to make the point that he was still in control.*[152]
>
> *As it turned out, over the next five years, City Market did very well and exceeded its earnings projections. It became a windfall for all of the shareholders. Not only did the shareholders earn the additional 5 percent of Dillon stock, but the stock value had increased tremendously in those five years.*
>
> *I doubt if Leo ever realized what he had done.*[153]

The warehouse was built in 1949 and filled a critical need in the supply chain. *Courtesy of Dan Prinster and the Joseph C. Prinster family.*

On July 28, 1969, the deal went through, and the headline on the front page of the *Daily Sentinel* announced: "City Market, Kansas Chain Announce Merger." The story read:

> *City Market, a 14-store chain of supermarkets based in Grand Junction is being merged with the Dillon Companies, a Kansas-based grocery chain. The merger, through which City Market becomes a wholly owned subsidiary of Dillon, was announced simultaneously this afternoon by City Market president Frank Prinster Jr. here and Dillon president, R.E. Dillon Jr. in Denver.*
>
> *City Market will continue to operate under the name with the same officers and store managers. Dillon becomes a member of the City Market*

board, and Prinster joins the Dillon board. The merger is the largest transaction involving a Western Slope firm announced in many years.[154]

Once again, City Market had changed. It had a new owner, new capacities and new opportunities. It was ready to greet the 1970s and march forward through the last quarter of the twentieth century.

Backstory Notes

Prior to the takeover, City Market had made its first venture outside the state of Colorado. One of the early ventures was to open a store in Farmington, New Mexico. This was not a successful endeavor, and after a year, the decision was made to close the store.

A store was also built in Moab, Utah, in 1962. It was nearly a disaster. By that time, the uranium boom had faded, but a large soda ash mine was being built, and it offered the prospect of growth in the area. The little store opened in Moab to great fanfare. Coming as a complete surprise to management, the construction of the mine and its facilities ended on the same day the store opened. The out-of-work construction workers all came to the grand opening, made large purchases and then left town. City Market discovered, too late, that it was left not only with a smaller customer base but also with a large number of returned checks marked "Account Closed." Management decided to stay in Moab anyway. In time, movie stars and movie companies discovered Moab, and the town eventually gained the reputation as the world capital for mountain biking and Jeep safaris. As the town grew, City Market grew with it.[155]

The *Daily Sentinel* article that announced the merger did not define the purchase price. "The Net Worth of the merger has not been calculated pending settlement of the final agreement," noted the *Sentinel.* Payment of the purchase price was to be made in shares of stock in Dillon Companies Inc., and the value of each share was determined by a formula tied to the closing price of Dillon stock on the New York Stock Exchange on a specific day. The "earn-out" that resulted from the meeting between Leo and Ace Dillon would be paid based on the number of shares paid to City Market shareholders at the time of the closing. When the earn-out shares were earned and paid, the market value of Dillon shares had increased. Curt Robinson estimates that the amount of the 5 percent earn-outs may have increased to as much as 20 percent over the original value.

The Presidents

There were only six presidents of the City Market Corporation. Five were Prinsters. The sixth and final was an ambitious young woman who earned her way from checker to president.

Leo Prinster

Leo was the only one of the four original brothers to serve as president of City Market. He was the de facto leader for many years, but he did not officially become president until City Market was incorporated in December 1954.[156] During his period of stewardship, from before 1939 until 1963, he pushed the expansion of City Market, beginning with the Montrose store in 1944. He was on board for the company's incorporation, hired the best minds in law and accounting to guide the company through its many changes, capitalized on the uranium and shale booms from the late 1940s to the early 1950s and added stores in Delta, Durango, Rifle and Cortez, as well as two new stores in Grand Junction. He paid for everything up front, thereby avoiding debt.[157]

Leo Prinster. *Author's collection.*

Leo ruled with an iron fist and resisted any suggestions for change coming from the younger generation.[158] Because of this and other reasons already explained, he was forced out of the company in 1963. When compared to his father, Joseph, however, Leo was just as hardworking, equally the risk-taker and to the core a captain of industry.

Frank Prinster Jr.

With Frank at the helm, the whole atmosphere changed within the corporation. Unlike his Uncle Leo, Frank was warm, understanding and—in the words of his cousin Jack—always a true gentleman.[159] However, he could be firm and hard-nosed when circumstances required. Educated as a scientist with a degree in chemistry from Creighton University, Frank aspired to become a doctor. He brought an insightful mind and orderly thought process to the business. During his nearly twenty years of leadership, the company enjoyed a fast-paced growth. City Market stores went from small neighborhood markets to massive venues offering thousands of products in sixty-thousand-square-foot buildings. Computers that allowed speed in recordkeeping and later in ordering and marketing were just being introduced to the grocery business.

The company opened its own bakery in Grand Junction to service the three Grand Junction stores, as well as the stores in Delta, Montrose, Rifle and Glenwood Springs. Venturing out of the state for the first time, the company opened stores in Moab, Utah, in 1962; in Farmington, New Mexico, and later Rawlins, Wyoming, in 1968; in Green River, Wyoming, in 1972; and in Rock Springs, Wyoming, in 1973. City Market replaced the store in Delta and opened new ones in Basalt, Breckenridge, Dillon, Avon, Gunnison and Aspen. After merging with Dillon, the company opened stores in Steamboat Springs, Cañon City and in the Eastgate Shopping Center in Grand Junction. They also replaced stores in Craig and Rifle.[160]

The expansion of the independent warehouse allowed all the stores to keep prices down and quality up. Most refreshing of all, Frank was always open to suggestions. He was supportive of other people's ideas, which in turn led to many industry innovations. He was a man of integrity, a great judge of character and a very good delegator.

Generous in his support of charitable efforts, Frank spearheaded a $2 million fundraising drive named Kind Hands for St. Mary's Hospital. He was a strong supporter of Partners, the Mesa State Foundation and Holy Family

Frank Prinster Jr. *Author's collection.*

School, among others. After his retirement in 1978, he quietly advanced the cause of the Marillac Clinic and so many other institutions that are key to serving the people of his community.

When Frank died in 1996, an editorial in the *Daily Sentinel* read, "Tens of thousands of people's lives were touched by the life of Frank J. Prinster.

Few worthy community projects were undertaken without his wholehearted support. What is impossible to quantify about Frank Prinster is the man's boundless humanity and profound decency."

Frank's legacy from his grandfather, Joseph (who never let a man go hungry) reflected this same generous humanity.[161]

Joe Prinster

Right after his graduation from high school, Joe enlisted in the United States Army. Joe told the enlisting sergeant that "he wanted to fight the Germans."[162] He was assigned to the 80th Infantry Division, 350th Regiment E, Company 1st Platoon. The 80th Infantry Division was part of the landing force following up after the Normandy invasion. There were forty-three men in the 1st Platoon, and Joe was one of eleven who returned. He was a decorated war hero. Joe immediately went to work for City Market. Although he didn't go to college, he was very proud of having apprenticed as a meat cutter with his father, Frank, and then overseeing the meat operations in all the stores. Joe was instrumental in introducing self-service meat cases in all the stores and, over time, bringing in other methods of processing, transporting and displaying meat. The level of meat-cutting skill that he learned from his father and his uncles is rarely found in today's modern supermarkets.

Joe was in his mid-fifties when he assumed the role of City Market president in 1978. At that time, the economy of the Western Slope was booming following the influx of major oil companies—Exxon in particular—that had moved in to develop the area's vast oil shale deposits.

These were heady times for businesses and citizens alike, and Joe's initial task was to capitalize on this explosive economic growth by accelerating the company's expansion in order to meet the market's demands. Additional stores came on line more rapidly than ever before, putting enormous pressure on warehousing, management and labor. But Joe was up to the task. He worked hand-in-glove with his brother Teo, his executive vice-president, to get things done. Four years later, all hell broke loose.

It will forever be recorded in the Western Slope's history as "Black Sunday." On the first Sunday in May 1982, Exxon moved out, overnight, with no prior warning, and it was soon followed by all the other major oil companies. Oil shale had once again proved too expensive to produce. Suddenly, it was a wild ride of extremes, from enormous prosperity to a local depression equal to the Great Depression of 1929.

Joe Prinster. *Courtesy of Dan Prinster and the Joseph C. Prinster family.*

About 20 percent of the regional population left, walking away from homes they could not sell. Businesses closed their doors, and bankruptcies rivaled foreclosures. Divorce skyrocketed, and suicide was not uncommon. U-Haul trailers were virtually impossible to find. A popular bumper sticker read, "Would the last one out of Grand Junction please turn out the lights?" It took major adaptability and ingenuity to survive.[163]

Hardest hit was Battlement Mesa and Exxon's Colony Oil Shale Development in nearby Parachute. City Market was preparing to build its largest supermarket in the state in Battlement Mesa. John Gaarde, then the City Market controller, said that a scaled-down version was renegotiated with local officials on the advice of Ace Dillon, who said, "Put something in there. If they pull out, we will, too." City Market's planned 55,000-square-foot store was reduced to 22,500 square feet.

During the store's grand opening on August 4, 1983, Garfield county commissioner Jim Drinkhouse cut the red ribbon and said, "We in Garfield County want to congratulate City Market and thank them for having faith in this area and county. I guarantee the rest of us do."[164] It was an optimistic speech at a time when optimism was a rare commodity. The entire company experienced layoffs and wage freezes, even wage rollbacks, something that had never occurred before. The Grand Junction stores did not make a profit for five years.

During that time, Joe stepped up to the plate and took a major leadership role with economic development efforts to bring in new businesses. He served as chairman of the Mesa County Economic Development Council and led its efforts to raise money to promote and underwrite new businesses and employers who would help rebuild the economic base.

In 1983, a major alteration occurred when City Market's parent company, Dillon Companies Inc., merged with Kroger Company. At the time, Kroger had more than 1,200 supermarkets in twenty states and five hundred drugstores that stretched from coast to coast. The impact of this merger would not be felt by City Market for five years. The company continued to operate independently as a wholly owned subsidiary.

In spite of economic hardships, City Market continued to revamp and grow. It added new stores in Hotchkiss in 1984 and Breckenridge in 1986. It replaced stores in Montrose, Glenwood Springs and Durango and built a store in Shiprock, New Mexico. In 1986, the company bought a chain of Circle Soopers Stores in Woodland Park, Carbondale, Kremmling, Buena Vista, Pagosa Springs, Conifer and Nederlands. That opened new markets. Between 1986 and 1987, the Steamboat Springs store was replaced, as was the store in Rock Springs, Wyoming.[165]

In 1987, after a forty-year career, Joe was ready to retire and turn the presidency over to his younger brother, Teo. As president, he'd seen the company through some of its worst years. Like his grandfather, Joseph, and his father and uncles before him, Joe kept the company alive and successful during those hard times by being resilient, innovative and willing to adapt to change. He is remembered by employees as a good man to know and a good president, someone who was friendly and down to earth, someone the employees could relate to and for whom they liked to work.

Teo Prinster

Teo was appointed president in 1987. He had worked hand in hand with Joe to steer the company successfully through three phenomenally difficult periods: the local oil shale bust recovery, the company-wide cutbacks and the restructuring that was required to stave off the corporate raiders who had targeted Kroger for a hostile takeover.

For most of the thirty-eight years after his graduation from the University of Utah in 1950 with a degree in banking and finance, Teo worked for his family's company. At the end of World War II, he served two years in the U.S. Marine Corps before embarking on his City Market career.

Teo Prinster. *Courtesy of Mrs. Carolyn Prinster.*

Teo worked in the Durango and Glenwood Springs stores and then managed the North Avenue store for eleven years. He managed the warehouse, worked as the general merchandiser and served as a director of the stores' operations.

It was in real estate, however, that Teo made his biggest contribution to City Market. He was made vice-president of real estate and development and quickly distinguished himself as having a keen eye for store sites and knowledgeable oversight of design and construction.

Teo's son Nick described his father's role and contribution to the company during his career:

> *He had faith in Colorado, that there would be a lot of growth. I know that once he and Joe started working up in the company, they were just definitely interested in getting the company to grow. Their philosophy was they needed to get into some of these smaller towns before the competitors got in there. Most of the big chains focused on building in densely populated urban areas, leaving smaller, less-profitable markets wide open. The Colorado areas that we operated in were rural; they would go unnoticed by large chains. We would put in a store that was fairly advanced for the community, and then we would* [employ] *a store manager who would be very community-minded and would make sure the store would grow with the community. That recipe would generally work.*[166]

Much like his grandfather Joseph, Teo had a knack for building and development. He oversaw much of the rapid expansion from the late 1960s until his retirement in 1990.

Teo had always worked closely with Joe. In the business community, they were known as "Mr. Inside and Mr. Outside." Teo's personality was more akin to his father Frank's, whereas Joe liked the limelight and was the outgoing one. Teo, as the behind-the-scenes operator, quietly assumed and performed many of the duties, responsibilities and functions of the office of presidency for Joe—by the time he was designated president, he had already "been there, done that."

In many ways, Teo was most like his own father and had the same deep feeling for his family. Teo expressed this in a letter to his brother Frank shortly before Frank's death in 1996. "As I get older, I have become more reflective and honest with the past. Tho still not totally correct, I can use hindsight more accurately on judgments than I did at the time things were happening. Family is so important in my life and yet I didn't always think so.

In fact I don't think I really understood that blood is thicker than water and appreciated my mother and father, brothers and sisters enough."[167]

Teo served as president for only three years, but his quiet and firm influence was felt long before his appointment to that position. Like his older brothers, Teo served his community in many leadership roles. He was a director on the board of St. Mary's Hospital and Club 20—a coalition of individuals, businesses, tribes and local governments in Colorado's twenty western counties—and was active in the Grand Junction Economic Partnership Council.

After Teo moved to Glenwood Springs, he dedicated his retirement years to tireless humanitarian work. He was a strong supporter of Grand Valley Catholic Outreach and Literacy Outreach, and he worked to support the Catholic Church in its many charitable causes. In 2007, Teo and his wife, Carolyn, were named Garfield County Humanitarians of the Year. Teo passed away on August 8, 2012.[168]

Tony Prinster

When Tony, Frank Jr.'s oldest son, graduated from high school, he stated in the school annual, "I do not know yet what career I will pursue in life. I know that I do not plan to settle in Grand Junction or go into the grocery business."

After Tony assumed the presidency of City Market in 1990, he recalled that statement. "I learned one of life's great lessons: Never say never." Tony would become the fifth Prinster to fill that role and also the last of the Prinsters to do so. It was his Uncle Teo who persuaded Tony to return to the family business.

Tony had worked throughout his childhood and teens in the stores, but like his Uncle Leo, he initially chose another career path. Tony attended the University of Notre Dame, where he studied English literature and business while spinning albums and reporting the news at the college radio station. Briefly he considered a career in radio and television but decided instead to study law. He returned to Colorado and earned his law degree at the University of Colorado in Boulder. After working a short time in Boulder, Tony was invited to join the law firm then known as Nelson, Hoskin and Groves (later, Nelson, Hoskin, Groves and Prinster).

For the next twenty years, Tony's practice focused on commercial and corporate law. He represented small businesses and worked on labor issues.

Tony Prinster. *Author's collection.*

He served in state and local bar associations' offices. When Tony's Uncle Teo became president, he asked Tony to rejoin the City Market fold in 1987.

"Sometimes you hit a plateau and you need a change," Tony said about his decision to accept the offer. "I decided it was better to risk a change than to turn down an opportunity and regret it later." Tony underwent intense tutelage as executive vice-president before becoming president in 1990. Teo expected that it would take at least seven years for Tony to learn the business. He was ready in three.

Phyllis Norris, who would succeed Tony as the first female president of the corporation, said, "Tony is a real businessman, and he brought us together out of chaos. His breadth of experience allows him to see the big picture and be flexible when needed."

John Gaarde, former controller of City Market, commented, "Tony probably absorbed more over the dinner table than anyone could hope."[169]

The years from 1990 to 2001 brought new challenges for Tony and the next generation of the City Market management team. When City Market merged with the Dillon Companies, the *Daily Sentinel* wrote on July 28, 1969, "City Market has a sales volume of $25 million and Dillon of $200 million." Twenty-five years later, by January 1994, the business had grown to more than forty stores, with annual sales exceeding $500 million.[170] By this time, City Market had become a huge business with large company problems and the challenges brought on by the new competitive environment.

The restructuring, cost control and consolidation of functions with the other Kroger divisions, especially King Soopers, continued, brought on by the "big-box stores," especially the behemoth, Walmart.

During Tony's ten-year tenure as president of City Market, expansion and growth continued. He oversaw replacements of the stores in Delta, Buena Vista, Dillon and Montrose and the construction of new stores in El Jebel, New Castle, Pagosa Springs, Eagle and Vail.[171] The Vail construction made headlines and history in 1997. One of the big hurdles to operating large grocery stores in resort communities has always been the availability (or lack thereof) of affordable housing for employees. To alleviate this problem, the company opted in the 1990s to build apartments for employees as part of the Avon store. In Vail, City Market not only built a new store but also built an entire housing complex in order to provide affordable housing for employees and their families.

Two years before Tony ended his tenure as president, on behalf of all City Market employees, he accepted the 1998 Chamber of Commerce Grand Junction Business of the Year Award that cited the contributions of the management teams and employees of money, sponsorships and volunteer time to numerous local nonprofit organizations, including United Way, the Kiwanis and Lions Clubs, St. Mary's Hospital, Hilltop House, Mesa County Economic Development Council and the American Cancer Society. In

1998 alone, City Market contributed more than $300,000 to Mesa County organizations.

In 1999, another major shift took place that would bring changes to City Market and end the Prinster family's physical involvement in the corporation. In 1999, Kroger shareholders overwhelmingly approved a merger with the Fred Meyers Corporation. This gave Kroger a presence in the western United States in states like Utah, California, Washington and Oregon. It would make Kroger the largest supermarket chain in the United States and help it compete with the supercenter stores, like Walmart, that were roaring into markets across the country.

By then, Fred Meyers had more than eight hundred locations—a variety of food, drug, and multi-department stores and one-stop shopping centers in twelve western states from Alaska to Texas and Montana to California. The corporation had a fleet of trucks and trailers and three major distribution centers. It employed eighty-five thousand people. Kroger operated 1,410 stores in twenty-four states under a number of different retail names and 797 convenience stores under six different names in fifteen states. It was another good match.

Before the merger could be finalized, the Federal Trade Commission, acting to maintain competition, required City Market to divest three of its forty-five stores. It sold the stores in Rock Springs and Green River, Wyoming, to the Fleming companies of Oklahoma City and the store in Price, Utah, to Albertsons.

"This was necessary in order to address the overlap between City Market and our new sister company, Salt Lake City-based Smith Food King," said Tony.

Kroger recognized that the merger would allow it to implement the new way supermarkets would now be run. The merger brought about more extensive changes. Kroger was required to cut costs by getting rid of unproductive stores and consolidating most of its functions. Its local warehousing was consolidated, along with the numerous tasks that City Market employees had always performed. These were now taken over by the Kroger Corporation, which meant layoffs and scaling down.

Breaking up seventy-five years of doing business the City Market way and turning almost all functions from buying, payroll, accounting and decision-making over to Kroger's Denver headquarters was a horrendous task. "Although such reduction is difficult and subject to continued speculation," said Tony at the time, "I see that the long-term plan is that City Market and

City Market personnel will continue. Although the structure has changed, City Market will continue to grow and remain a force in Western Colorado."

Tony retired in 2001 in his sixties.

Phyllis Norris

After becoming City Market's first female president, the question Phyllis was asked most often was, "Which Prinster are you related to?" It was a natural assumption. Little did people realize that Phyllis had begun working for City Market thirty years earlier as a part-time checker for $2.75 per hour.

"I was thrilled when they hired me," recalled Phyllis, who at the time was a twenty-three-year-old mother of three. "Everyone wanted to work for City Market back then. I thought I had the best job in the world. I still feel that way."

Compared to today, City Market was a very different place to work in the 1970s. Only women worked the checkout counters, and only men worked the floor. There were no scanners or computers, just keyboards. When employees weighed produce, they had to calculate the price in their heads and know the price of each item. They were regularly tested on this. Fortunately, they didn't have a lot of produce in those days because everything was seasonal. The only produce that remained on the shelf year round was lettuce and tomatoes.

After a year working as a checker, Phyllis noticed that there was an opening to stock drugs and beauty aids. She applied and got the job. No woman had ever worked the floors before in any of City Market's sixteen stores. The men didn't like it.

"At first, none of the men would help me," said Phyllis. "They wouldn't even show me how to properly open cases. I was always cutting my fingers. It also was a struggle to move big boxes. Finally Ray Patten took pity on me and showed me how things were done. Eventually the other men started helping me too."

Becoming the first woman to work the floor put Phyllis on the path to becoming the first woman in the City Market chain to break one male barrier after another. She was smart, ambitious and eager to learn. She was not afraid to work as hard as, or harder than, any man in the company. The Prinster presidents from Joe to Tony saw her potential and encouraged her to move forward with each passing year. She was the first female assistant manager, the first female manager, the first female district

Phyllis Norris. *Courtesy of Phyllis Norris.*

manager, the first female vice-president (under Tony) and, finally, the first female president—not only in the City Market chain but also in the entire

Kroger Corporation. She had worked on every level and knew every detail about how to run a big company.

By 2000, she had earned her place at the top. The merger with Fred Meyers was the biggest hurdle. As Tony's vice-president, she helped him restructure the company, breaking it down and rebuilding it. Everything she had worked so hard to learn over the years was no longer needed under the new corporate structure. From marketing to hiring, expansion to ordering, these functions were now decided on and done by corporate in Denver or Cincinnati.

"It was hard," said Phyllis, "really hard. For instance 'just-in-time' ordering took the place of what we had always done manually. The minute an item went off the shelf, it was immediately ordered electronically, packaged, and shipped to the warehouse in Denver and then to us."

During the transition of closing down operations, the truckers and warehouse employees were particularly affected. They all were going to lose their jobs since warehousing would now be handled in Denver.

"It was really hard to convince those people to stay on and help with the transition when they knew their jobs were being terminated," Phyllis said. "Those who stayed with us while we downsized got a very substantial severance package. We were up-front with everyone. We told them we hoped to downsize gradually over three or four years, but suddenly we were told to do it now. We had one year. It was really rough."

As president, it was her job to make City Market remain City Market and to keep things running smoothly in all the stores. This meant a lot of traveling. The store in Shiprock, New Mexico, on the Navajo reservation was one of her most interesting stores to visit. Everything there was run differently than anywhere else. "The Navajos don't eat lamb, only mutton, so we shipped whole sides of mutton, which they chopped rather than cut, in the way the Navajos preferred it," Phyllis said. "Because these people live out in the middle of nowhere without electricity, they bought a lot of Spam—more Spam was sold there than in any of the stores in the entire corporation from coast to coast."

For a while, they almost put the medicine man on the payroll. "The manager in Shiprock was having problems with pigeons flying into the store, so he put fake owls all around the store to scare them off," Phyllis recalled. "After having done this, he returned the next morning and found his employees waiting outside the store, refusing to go in. They have a superstition about owls [they portend death]. So he not only had to take down all the fake owls but bring the medicine man in to purify the store before anyone would go back to work. The medicine man was called in again when their baker died in a car accident. The employees were certain his spirit was hanging around the store. When a snake crawled into the back room one day, the employees promptly removed themselves again and wouldn't return until after the medicine man had performed a special ceremony. We could write a whole book on that Shiprock store," Phyllis laughed.

She has many other memories. She remembered when Leo would come into the store and stand right behind the checkers. This made them nervous, and he knew it. He did it to Phyllis one day, and she just turned around and said, "Mr. Prinster, would you mind standing over there? I'm feeling crowded." He moved. She also remembered how the retired Frank Sr. came daily into the Eastgate store and checked the sale items. Some he marked back up, others down even further. "After he left, we'd put things back the way they were." Both Leo and Frank Sr. often helped themselves to items without paying. "We figured they had earned the right, so nothing was said about it."

As president, Phyllis met regularly with corporate in Denver and was told that things were to be done a certain way, "even though they had little concept or understanding of what our customers on the Western Slope expected. It was a battle to help City Market stay City Market," she said. "But times had changed, and we knew that we would not have survived if we hadn't restructured our company."

Phyllis served as president for ten years. Before she retired, she was notified that another restructuring was about to take place. She stayed on long enough to complete the restructuring and support the associates.

After retirement in 2011, Phyllis was elected to the Grand Junction City Council.

After the Kroger Merger

During the twenty years following the merger with Kroger, Dillon Companies Inc. and City Market Inc. progressed through multiple structural changes in order to adjust to economic times and meet competitive demands. The corporate entity City Market Inc. was dissolved, and the assets, including the name "City Market," were assumed into the Kroger corporate structure. Today, the operations of City Market are directed from King Soopers in Denver and Kroger in Cincinnati, Ohio.

EPILOGUE

In June 1995, our family traveled to the land on which my great-grandfather had walked 141 years before. There were six of us: my wife, Sally; our daughter Stephanie and her husband, Jon Mottram; and our daughters Sarah and Antonia ("Nia"). We met family members we never would have known had it not been for the persistence of our distant cousin Tayana Pruenster and the letter she sent on July 23, 1992, to Joseph C. Prinster in Tempe, Arizona. The journey was a memorable and profoundly moving experience.

We arrived in Munich, Germany, on June 16, and after two days, we took the train to Innsbruck, Austria. Innsbruck is a magnificent city surrounded by high snowcapped mountains, with clear blue skies and fresh mountain air. Reminiscent of Aspen, Colorado, it is populated by many hikers in the summer and skiers in the winter. I could see immediately why my great-grandfather Joseph spoke longingly of Innsbruck and wanted to return. After two days, we boarded a train for South Tyrol.

The train climbed the Brenner Pass through green valleys, its hillsides blanketed with spruce trees. We passed through channels cut in the deep snowdrifts that still lingered from winter. It could have been a trip over Vail Pass and down through the Vail Valley. Our destination was Bolzano (in German, *Bozen*), the gateway to the mighty Dolomites to the east and the verdant Alto Adige to the west. We planned to travel to Merano (in German, *Meran*) twenty miles to the northwest and then four miles up the Passeier Valley to Riffian.

Before we left Innsbruck, I was apprehensive. We were to meet total strangers, yet they were relatives. Our only contact was a twenty-six-year-old woman with whom I had spoken once by phone and exchanged letters a few times. "Is this crazy?" I wondered. Would we relate to each other? Do they speak English? What if we can't get beyond simple gestures and searching for single words in a bilingual dictionary? Were we about to experience a colossal embarrassment?

We crossed Brenner Pass to South Tyrol, Italy, and descended the steep inclines to the valley floor. I found myself comparing this ride to the descent of the narrow gauge from Silverton to Durango, Colorado: towering snowcapped peaks, steep mountain gorges, tumbling mountain streams and tight switchbacks.

When the train pulled into Bolzano, I felt like we had stepped into a painting from the 1920s. The station was an old stone building facing tree-lined cobblestone streets, with multicolored tile roofs jutting above the trees and an old dry fountain in front of the station building. It could have been a scene from Hemingway's *A Farewell to Arms.*

Only a few passengers disembarked with us. There was no crowd waiting to board the train or greet arriving passengers. We gathered our bags from the overhead racks and stumbled off the train.

I could feel my heart begin to pound as my apprehension grew. No use looking for a familiar face. We didn't know anyone. Then, from across the platform, a young woman hurried toward us. She was tall, with very dark brown hair, attractive, with a magnetic smile. She wore a blue and white striped summer blouse and carried a large bouquet of flowers.

"Tony?" she asked in perfect English. "It's Tayana." Instantly we felt welcome, and my anxiety evaporated. We could not have asked for a better tour guide. Tayana was a ray of sunshine, a breath of fresh spring air. Her English was only slightly accented. Her voice had a lilt, almost as if she were singing, not speaking. That lilt seemed to carve out each word with care. It was delightful to hear. She had prepared an itinerary for each day of our five-day visit.

After saying hello to Tayana's family, we walked through Riffian and stopped at the parish Church of the Seven Sorrows of Mary, where some of our ancestors lay in the graveyard. We continued walking to the Passer River, stopping along the way to meet Tayana's Uncle Florian and his wife, Maria, who live at Obereggelehof. Tayana then took us to the Hotel Kreuzwirt, the charming little hotel where we would stay.

The author met Tayana Pruenster (second from left) for the first time at the train station in Bolzano, Italy. *Author's collection.*

The next day, we visited the various places of the Pruensters' origins. We met Alois; his wife, Cilli; and their son, Stefan, at Ausserpircherhof in Vernuer. This is the site of the original farmhouse where my great-grandfather Joseph had been born in 1854.

Alois and I are the same age. He was born in January 1941, two months before my birth. He is the direct descendant of Johann, my great-grandfather's older brother. He inherited the farm from his father, who had inherited it from his father, Johann.

First sons had lived on this farm for several centuries. It is in a beautiful setting, perched on a steep slope that leads down to the Passer River at the floor of the valley. Each first son had spent his life working the farm. Alois continued that tradition and had spent his life tilling the fields and attending his herd of ten dairy cows.

As beautiful as it is, the harsh demands of that existence were apparent. As we said goodbye to Alois and Cilli, two thoughts occurred to me: my great-grandfather did not inherit the farm and, for many years, had a difficult and challenging life in America. But upon reflection, I think he was the lucky one. Then, I thought, if Joseph had inherited that farm, could I have been the person on that farm instead of Alois?

Alois Pruenster maintaining the hay fields at the place of Joseph Prinster's birth. *Author's collection.*

I had a lot more to reflect on after our visit ended. I thought about my great-grandfather, who he was, what he did, what he must have been like and what he accomplished.

He left home at age eighteen with no money, yet somehow he secured passage on the ship *Hammonia* and found his way to the port of New York. He was a risk-taker and probably a good planner. He was smart enough to make his way to a new world and learn to read and write a new language. His penchant for taking risks continued throughout his life and carried him from New York to the packinghouses of Cincinnati, where he labored for ten years and learned the butcher's trade. After applying for citizenship, he went to the gold mines of Cripple Creek and from there to La Junta, where he started multiple businesses, bought real estate, incurred debt, suffered setbacks, enjoyed successes and raised and supported a large family.

His obituary in 1929 described him as an "indefatigable worker who possessed the qualities that spell success. He was energetic and progressive and lived to see materialized much that he had visualized for La Junta and for himself. Mr. Prinster was a devoted family man and while the joy of

The flag of South Tyrol was the last sight as the author's train left Bolzano and proceeded to the summit of the Brenner Pass. *Author's collection.*

accomplishment in each day's work constituted much of the happiness of his life, probably his greatest happiness lay within the four walls of his home."

His wife, Millie, wrote to Joseph's family in Riffian and described his energy. She even wondered if he was actually seventy-five when he died. She wrote, "He was always kind to people. People were known to say that 'No one ever went hungry when Old Joe was around.'" That is a monumental tribute to a once-penniless immigrant.

We departed Riffian on Sunday, June 25, 1995. It was a glorious, bright, early summer morning. As the train left Bolzano and started back up Brenner Pass to Innsbruck, we could see the bright red and white banners lofting lightly in the breeze. They were flying from church steeples and tall buildings in celebration of a special Tyrolean holiday, Sacred Heart Sunday. Their vivid colors stood out against the background of the lush, green Tyrolean mountainside.

The experience of our visit consumed my thoughts. I wondered about Joseph and his origins. What were his ideas and motivations when he left this valley? Could he have imagined at age eighteen what his life would bring or what he wanted to accomplish? He could not have known or guessed that someday it would be said of him, "He lived to see much of what he visualized for himself."

As we headed home, I thought of the business to which I would return, a large retail company with several thousand employees, forty-five stores, warehouses and trucks—a large enterprise. The seeds of that enterprise were planted by my great-grandfather Joseph.

I doubt if he visualized all that he accomplished in his own life. He would never have imagined all that his succeeding generations would accomplish, either. As I reflected on these things, I knew that at some time and in some way, I had to tell his whole story—his story—and now I have.

APPENDIX I

CITY MARKET STORES

Historical Stores

Location	**Opened/Built**
La Junta (116 West Second Street)	1921
Grand Junction (North Fourth Street)	1924
Grand Junction (Fourth and Rood Avenue)	1939
Montrose	1944
Delta	1945
Glenwood Springs	1948
Grand Junction (Ninth and North Avenue)	1950
Durango (Original #6)	1950
Grand Junction (Fourth and Grand Avenue)	1956

Current List of City Market Stores

Note: 400s indicate current store numbers. A break in the number sequence indicates that no store has been given that number. Information for the historical stores was taken from old files, lists and notes and may contain some inaccuracies. A City Market was opened in Framington, New Mexico, circa 1966 but was operated for only a short time. City Market (First and Orchard) was originally acquired from Brach's Market in 1960.

Store #	Location	Year Built/ Opened
401	Grand Junction (Highway 50 South)	1982
402	Ship Rock, New Mexico	1986
403	Montrose (South Townsend)	1986
404	Delta	1991
405	Glenwood Springs	1986
406	Durango (Town Plaza Shopping Center)	1986
407	Rifle (closed)	1954
408	Cortez	1981
	Cortez (original)	1956
409	Grand Junction (First and Orchard; closed)	1968
410	Moab, Utah	1989
	Moab (original)	1962
411	Basalt (closed)	1965
412	Rawlyns, Wyoming	1980
413	Fruita	1979
	Fruita (original; was Walton's Market)	1969
414	Steamboat Springs	1987
	Steamboat Springs (original)	1974
415	Craig	1973
	Original (Bill's Market)	1964
	Craig (original)	1970
416	Aspen	1970
417	Canyon City	1977
418	Grand Junction (closed; East Gate)	1974
419	Gunnison	1990
	Gunnison (original)	1976
420	Dillon	1998
	Silverthorne (closed)	1976
421	Durango (North Main)	1978
422	Alamosa	1977

423	Green River, Wyoming (closed)	1972
424	Rock Springs, Wyoming (closed)	1973
425	Grand Junction (32 Rood)	1980
426	Avon	1980
427	Price, Utah (closed)	1981
428	Battlement Mesa (closed)	1983
429	Hotchkiss	1984
430	Breckenridge	1986
431	Woodland Park	1986
432	Grand Junction (200 Rood)	1990
433	El Jebel	1995
434	Eagle	1997
435	Carbondale	1986
436	Conifer (closed)	1986
437	Buena Vista	1995
438	Pagosa Springs (closed)	1986
439		
440	Montrose (South)	1996
441	New Castle	1997
442	Vail	1997
443	Rifle	2003
444		
445	Pagosa Springs	1997
446	Granby	2004
447		
448		
449		
450		
451	Grand Junction (24 Rood)	2011

APPENDIX II

EXHIBITS

Joseph Pruenster Birth Certificate

Kronland: Tirol (Tyrol)   (Diocese) Diözese: Trient

Polit. Bezirk: Meran (Stadt mit eig. Stat.)   Pfarre: Riffian

Nr. 11.

(Birth) (Baptism)

Geburts- und Taufschein

(Zeugnis)

2

Aus den hiesigen Geburts- und Taufregistern Tom. IV. pag. 186. wird hiemit amtlich bezeugt, daß

in (Ort, Straße, Nr.): beim Aufrerpircher in Vernuer, Pfarren. Gem. Riffian

am (Datum): 24 November

des Jahres Eintausend acht hundert fünfzig vier

(in Ziffern): 1854.

geboren und am (Datum und Jahr): selben Tage

vom hochwürdigen Herrn: Cooperator Josef Sarch

nach römisch-katholischem (Roman Catholic) Ritus getauft wurde das

Kind (Child) (Vor- und Zuname): Prünster Josef.

ehelicher (unehelich) Sohn (Son) — Tochter — des

Vaters (Vor- und Zuname, Charakter, Religion, Wohnort, Zuständigkeitsort):

Prünster Josef Aufrerpircher in Vernuer, Riffian, Röm. Kath.

und der

Mutter (Vor- und Zuname rc. — Ebenso von den Eltern derselben):

Grüner Maria dessen ersten Ehefrau Röm. Kath. (Roman Catholic)

Paten: Prünster Anton, Rössl in Riffian

Urkund dessen die eigenhändige Unterschrift des Gefertigten und das beigedrückte Amtssiegel.

Riffian, am 5. Jaenner (January) 1911.

(L. S.)   Seb. Platt, Pfr.

F.B. PFARRAMT RIFFIAN BEI MERAN

Druck und Verlag von F. Landt's Buchdruckerei, Meran.

Marriage License of Joseph Prinster and Bohemilla "Millie" Kroboth

STATE OF KANSAS,
COUNTY OF SEDGWICK,

Office of the Probate Judge of said County.

BE IT REMEMBERED, That on the 18th *day of* October *A. D. 188*9, *there was issued from the office of said Probate Judge, a Marriage License, of which the following is a true copy:*

Marriage License.

Sedgwick County, State of Kansas.

October 18 1889

To Any Person Authorized by Law to Perform the Marriage Ceremony. Greeting:

You are hereby authorized to join in Marriage
Joseph F Prinster of La Junta Col *aged* 30 *years, and*
Miss Millie Kroboth of Wichita Kansas *aged* 19 *years,*
and of this License you will make due return to my office within thirty days.

[SEAL.] W. F. Buckner Probate Judge.

And which said Marriage License was afterwards, to-wit: on the 21st *day of* October *A. D. 18*89
returned to said Probate Judge, with the following certificate endorsed thereon, to-wit:

STATE OF KANSAS, } ss.
COUNTY OF SEDGWICK,

I, Rev John Lovrnich a Catholic Priest *do hereby certify that in accordance with the authorization of the within License, I did on the* 19th *day of* October *A. D. 188*9 *at* Wichita,
in said County, join and unite in Marriage the within named Joseph F Prinster
and Millie Kroboth

Witness my hand and seal the day and year above written.

Rev John Lovrnich

Attest .... Probate Judge.

JOSEPH PRINSTER CITIZENSHIP CERTIFICATE

Published by SIEBERT & LILLEY, Blank Book Manufacturers and Legal Blank Publishers, Opera House Building Columbus, O.

UNITED STATES OF AMERICA.

DECLARATION OF INTENTION.

Be it Remembered, That on the 25th day of March in the year of our Lord One Thousand Eight Hundred and Eighty four, personally appeared before me, R. M. Ditty Judge and ex-officio Clerk of the Probate Court within and for the County of Highland, and State of Ohio, Joseph Prinster an alien, a native of Austria and makes report of himself for naturalization; who, being duly sworn according to law, on his oath doth declare and say that it is bona fide his

INTENTION TO BECOME A CITIZEN OF THE UNITED STATES,

and to renounce forever all allegiance and fidelity to any Foreign Prince, Potentate, State or Sovereignty, and particularly to Francis Joseph Emperor of Austria whose subject he is.

ATTEST: R. M. Ditty Probate Judge and ex-officio Clerk.

The State of Ohio, Highland County, ss.

I, R. M. Ditty, Judge and ex-officio Clerk of the Probate Court within and for said County, do hereby certify that the foregoing is a true copy of the original entry of Declaration entered and remaining of record in this office.

WITNESS my hand and the seal of the Probate Court, at [illegible] Ohio, this 25th day of March A. D. 188–

R. M. Ditty Probate Judge and ex-officio Clerk.

By Cas Wright Deputy Clerk.

JOSEPH PRINSTER NATURALIZATION CERTIFICATE

No. 1650045

To be given to the person Naturalized.

THE UNITED STATES OF AMERICA

CERTIFICATE OF NATURALIZATION

Petition, Volume 3 Number 250

Description of holder: Age, 71 years; height, 6 feet, 2 inches; color, White; complexion, Medium; color of eyes, Brown; color of hair, Grey; visible distinguishing marks, None

Name, age and place of residence of wife [redacted]

Names, ages and places of residence of minor children Clarence, 19 yrs., Denver, Colorado

ORIGINAL

State of Colorado
County of Otero } SS: Joseph Frank Prinster (Signature of holder)

Be it remembered, that Joseph Frank Prinster then residing at number 401 Raton Avenue Street, City of La Junta State of Colorado, who previous to his naturalization was a subject of Italy, having applied to be admitted a citizen of the United States of America pursuant to law, and at a Regular term of the District Court of Otero County held at La Junta, Colo. on the 9th day of June in the year of our Lord nineteen hundred and Twenty-five the court having found that the petitioner had resided continuously within the United States for at least five years and in this State for at least one year immediately preceding the date of the filing of his petition, and that said petitioner intends to reside permanently in the United States, had in all respects complied with the law in relation thereto, and that he was entitled to be so admitted, it was thereupon ordered by the said court that he be admitted as a citizen of the United States of America.

In testimony whereof the seal of said court is hereunto affixed on the 9th day of June in the year of our Lord nineteen hundred and Twenty-five and of our Independence the one hundred and Forty-ninth

Clarence B. Crow
CLERK DISTRICT COURT
(Official character of attestor)

DEPARTMENT OF LABOR

Appendix II

Pruenster/Prinster Family Tree

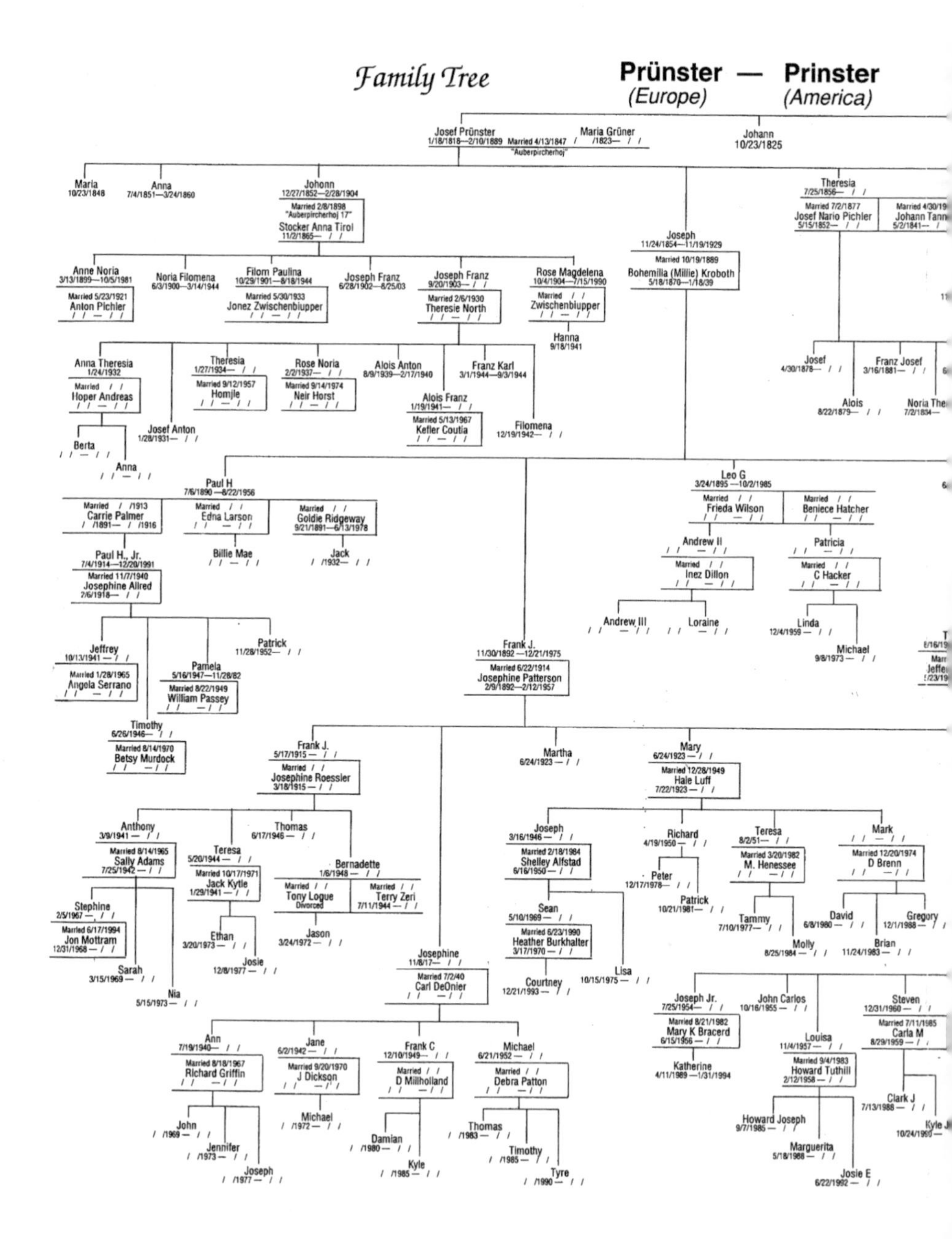

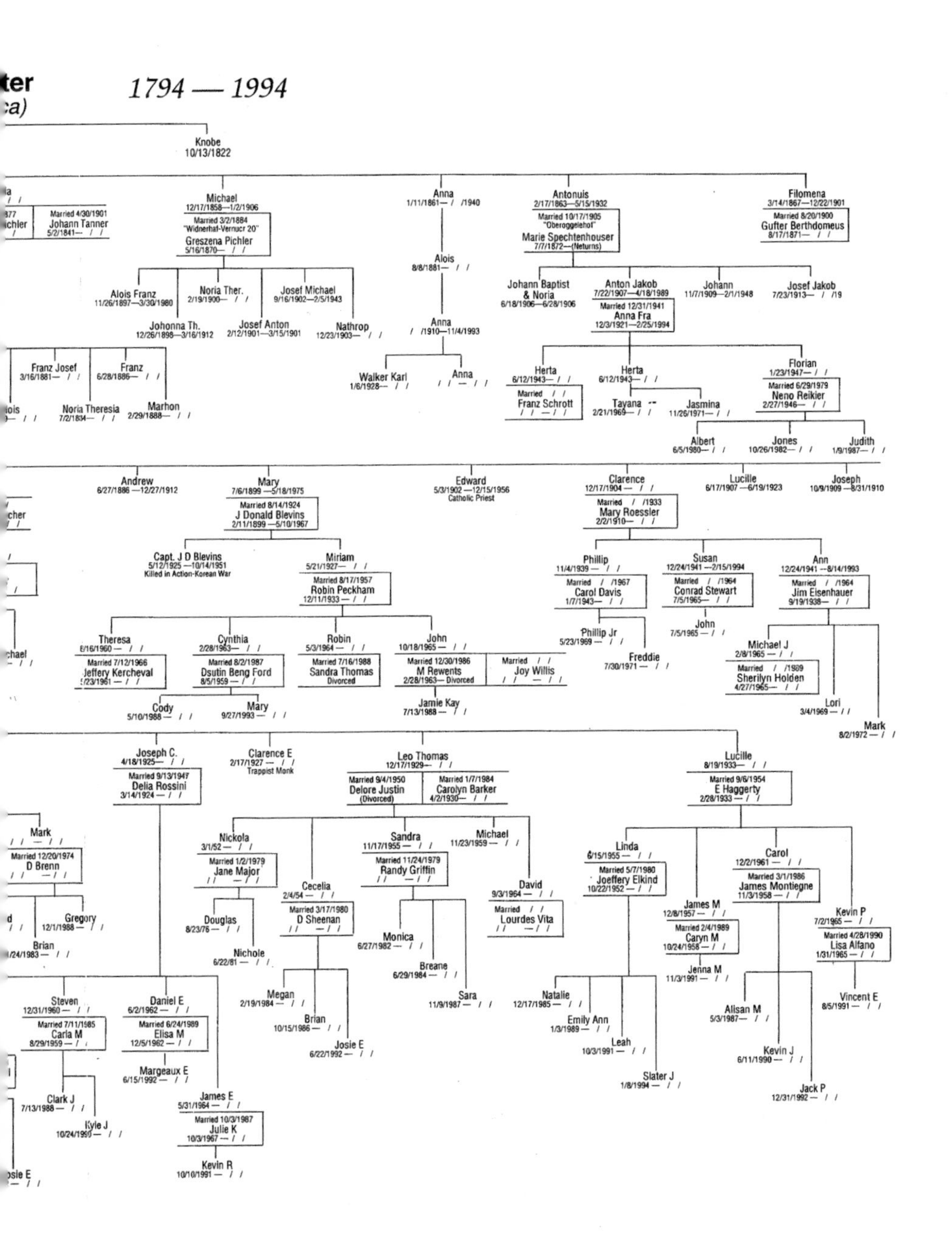

ter
ca)
1794 — 1994
Knobe
10/13/1822
Married 4/30/1901
Johann Tanner
5/2/1841— / /
Michael
12/17/1858—1/2/1906
Married 3/2/1884
"Widnerhaf-Vernucr 20"
Greszena Pichler
5/16/1870— / /
Anna
1/11/1861— / /1940
Antonuis
2/17/1863—5/15/1932
Married 10/17/1905
"Oberoggelehof"
Marie Spechtenhouser
7/7/1872—(Neturns)
Filomena
3/14/1867—12/22/1901
Married 8/20/1900
Gufter Berthdomeus
8/17/1871— / /
Alois Franz
11/26/1897—3/30/1980
Johonna Th.
12/26/1898—3/16/1912
Noria Ther.
2/19/1900— / /
Josef Anton
2/12/1901—3/15/1901
Josef Michael
9/16/1902—2/5/1943
Nathrop
12/23/1903— / /
Alois
8/8/1881— / /
Anna
/ /1910—11/4/1993
Walker Karl
1/6/1928— / /
Anna
/ / — / /
Johann Baptist
& Noria
6/18/1906—6/28/1906
Anton Jakob
7/22/1907—4/18/1989
Married 12/31/1941
Anna Fra
12/3/1921—2/25/1994
Johann
11/7/1909—2/1/1948
Josef Jakob
7/23/1913— / /19
Herta
6/12/1943— / /
Married / /
Franz Schrott
/ / — / /
Herta
6/12/1943— / /
Tayana
2/21/1969— / /
Jasmina
11/26/1971— / /
Florian
1/23/1947— / /
Married 6/29/1979
Neno Reikier
2/27/1946— / /
Albert
6/5/1980— / /
Jones
10/26/1982— / /
Judith
1/9/1987— / /
Franz Josef
3/16/1881— / /
Franz
6/28/1886— / /
Noria Theresia
7/2/1884— / /
Marhon
2/29/1888— / /
Andrew
6/27/1886—12/27/1912
Mary
7/6/1899—5/18/1975
Married 8/14/1924
J Donald Blevins
2/11/1899—5/10/1967
Edward
5/3/1902—12/15/1956
Catholic Priest
Clarence
12/17/1904— / /
Married / /1933
Mary Roessler
2/2/1910— / /
Lucille
6/17/1907—6/19/1923
Joseph
10/9/1909—8/31/1910
Capt. J D Blevins
5/12/1925—10/14/1951
Killed in Action-Korean War
Miriam
5/21/1927— / /
Married 8/17/1957
Robin Peckham
12/11/1933— / /
Phillip
11/4/1939— / /
Married / /1967
Carol Davis
1/7/1943— / /
Susan
12/24/1941—2/15/1994
Married / /1964
Conrad Stewart
7/5/1965— / /
Ann
12/24/1941—8/14/1993
Married / /1964
Jim Eisenhauer
9/19/1938— / /
Theresa
6/16/1960— / /
Married 7/12/1966
Jeffery Kercheval
5/23/1961— / /
Cynthia
2/28/1963— / /
Married 8/2/1987
Dsutin Beng Ford
8/5/1959— / /
Robin
5/3/1964— / /
Married 7/16/1988
Sandra Thomas
Divorced
John
10/18/1965— / /
Married 12/30/1986
M Rewents
2/28/1963—Divorced
Married / /
Joy Willis
/ / — / /
Phillip Jr
5/23/1969— / /
Freddie
7/30/1971— / /
John
7/5/1965— / /
Michael J
2/8/1965— / /
Married / /1989
Sherilyn Holden
4/27/1965— / /
Lori
3/4/1969— / /
Mark
8/2/1972— / /
Cody
5/10/1988— / /
Mary
9/27/1993— / /
Jamie Kay
7/13/1988— / /
Joseph C.
4/18/1925— / /
Married 9/13/1947
Delia Rossini
3/14/1924— / /
Clarence E
2/17/1927— / /
Trappist Monk
Leo Thomas
12/17/1929— / /
Married 9/4/1950
Delore Justin
(Divorced)
Married 1/7/1984
Carolyn Barker
4/2/1930— / /
Lucille
8/19/1933— / /
Married 9/6/1954
E Haggerty
2/28/1933— / /
Mark
/ / — / /
Married 12/20/1974
D Brenn
/ / — / /
Gregory
12/1/1988— / /
Brian
/24/1983— / /
Nickola
3/1/52— / /
Married 1/2/1979
Jane Major
/ / — / /
Cecelia
2/4/54— / /
Married 3/17/1980
D Sheenan
/ / — / /
Sandra
11/17/1955— / /
Married 11/24/1979
Randy Griffin
/ / — / /
Michael
11/23/1959— / /
David
9/3/1964— / /
Married / /
Lourdes Vita
/ / — / /
Linda
6/15/1955— / /
Married 5/7/1980
Joeffery Elkind
10/22/1952— / /
James M
12/8/1957— / /
Married 2/4/1989
Caryn M
10/24/1958— / /
Carol
12/2/1961— / /
Married 3/1/1986
James Montiegne
11/3/1958— / /
Kevin P
7/2/1965— / /
Married 4/28/1990
Lisa Alfano
1/31/1965— / /
Douglas
8/23/76— / /
Nichole
6/22/81— / /
Megan
2/19/1984— / /
Brian
10/15/1986— / /
Josie E
6/22/1992— / /
Monica
6/27/1982— / /
Breane
6/29/1984— / /
Sara
11/9/1987— / /
Natalie
12/17/1985— / /
Emily Ann
1/3/1989— / /
Leah
10/3/1991— / /
Slater J
1/8/1994— / /
Jenna M
11/3/1991— / /
Alisan M
5/3/1987— / /
Kevin J
6/11/1990— / /
Jack P
12/31/1992— / /
Vincent E
8/5/1991— / /
Steven
12/31/1960— / /
Married 7/11/1985
Carla M
8/29/1959— / /
Daniel E
6/2/1962— / /
Married 6/24/1989
Elisa M
12/5/1962— / /
Margeaux E
6/15/1992— / /
James E
5/31/1964— / /
Married 10/3/1987
Julie K
10/3/1967— / /
Kevin R
10/10/1991— / /
Clark J
7/13/1988— / /
Kyle J
10/24/1990— / /
osie E
— / /

NOTES

Part I

1. *La Junta Tribune*, "Death of a Pioneer," obituary for Joseph F. Prinster, November 1929.
2. Millie Prinster letter, La Junta, Colorado, April 10, 1930, addressed to "My dear relatives.
3. Memo from Mary Blevins files, handwritten, captioned "Grandfather Prinster," undated and unsigned, author unknown. Document no. 20 in author's files; letter to Joseph C. Prinster Jr. from Millie Vedder, January 6, 1968. Born Amelia Josephine Simon on December 21, 1888, Millie Vedder was the niece of Millie Prinster.
4. Letter from Tayana Pruenster to Joseph Prinster, July 23, 1992.
5. Family history recounted in an e-mail from Tayana Pruenster to Anthony Prinster, March 7, 2010.
6. Letter from Tayana Pruenster to Frank Prinster, September 12, 1994; Tyrol file, July 2013, Renate Abram, "A Summary on Tyrol, South Tyrol," translated by Paul Andrew Hammond.
7. Tayana Pruenster e-mail, March 7, 2010.
8. Letter from Tayana Pruenster to Frank Prinster, December 17, 1993.
9. History of South Tyrol and comments prepared by Tayana Pruenster, June 10, 1995.
10. Letter from Tayana Pruenster to Frank Prinster, December 17, 1993; letter from Tayana Pruenster to Frank Prinster, February 8, 1995; Anthony F. Prinster, "A Brief Family History," written in 1996 from notes accumulated after first trip to Riffian, Italy.
11. Tayana Pruenster e-mail correspondence to Anthony Prinster, February 2, 2013.
12. Tayana Pruenster e-mail correspondence to Anthony Prinster, March 7, 2010.
13. Tayana Pruenster and Renate Abram e-mail correspondence with Anthony Prinster, January 29, 2013; Tayana Pruenster e-mail correspondence with Anthony Prinster, January 25, 2013; "A Summary on Tyrol, South Tyrol," written in July 2013 by Renate Abram, translated by Paul Andrew Hammond.
14. Facts from the Ships List website, www.theshipslist.com.
15. *New York Daily Times*, August 4, 1855; the Ships List, theshipslist.com.
16. Castle Garden, the Battery Conservancy, castlegarden.org.
17. Millie Prinster letter, La Junta, Colorado, April 10, 1930, addressed to "My dear relatives."
18. Liz Gray, "Porkopolis: Cincinnati's Pork-Producing Past," Frontdoor, March 12, 2009, http://www.frontdoor.com/places/porkopolis-cincinnatis-pork-producing-past.
19. United States of America, Declaration of Intention, Joseph Prinster, Probate Court at Hillsboro, Ohio, March 25, 1884.

20. William D. Keel, "The German Heritage of Kansas: An Introduction," University of Kansas, copyright 2000–2005, found at Swiss Mennonite Cultural and Historical Association website, http://www.swissmennonite.org/feature_archive/2002/200201.html.

21. *Daily Sentinel*, "The Story of Prinster Brothers Typical of American Business Life Success," obituary for Joseph F. Prinster, possibly August 1950; interview with Joseph C. Prinster, September 17, 2008. Information for this and other chapters supplied through personal interviews with and statements from Joseph C. Prinster Sr. Eleven such interviews between Joe and the author took place between September 17, 2008, and September 21, 2011. Recordings and transcriptions are preserved and available.

22. *La Junta Tribune*, December 29, 1887; April 15, 1888; April 12, 1888; June 7, 1888; September 13, 1888; June 27, 1889; January 14, 1890.

23. Letter to Joseph C. Prinster Jr. from Millie Vedder, January 6, 1968. Born Amelia Josephine Simon on December 21, 1888, she was the niece of Millie Prinster. Declaration of Intent for Citizenship, Joseph D. Kroboth, U.S. District Court, Denver, Colorado, September 22, 1939.

24. Letter from Lenore Simpson to Mary Blevins, July 16, 1958; "S I M O N," an essay written by Duane F. Gersienberger of San Antonio, Texas, dated Christmas 1988, in author's files, designated document no. 44. Mr. Gersienberger is the husband of Millie Vedder's youngest daughter, Ruthelma Millie.

25. Marriage license of Joseph F. Prinster and Miss Millie Kroboth, October 18, 1889, Sedgwick County, Kansas, issued on October 24, 1889, Index/Record no. 636.

26. Warranty deed, Thomas F. Miller to Joseph F. Prinster, November 29, 1889, reception no. 577, Book 5, page 127, Records of the Clerk and Recorder, Otero County, Colorado; warranty deed, Jacob H. Cardiff to Joseph F. Prinster, December 16, 1889, reception no. 624, Book 5, page 141; warranty deed, Joseph F. Prinster to Millie Prinster, October 1, 1892, reception no. 4362, Book 17, page 376.

27. *History of the State of Colorado*, vol. 4, by Frank Hall for the Rocky Mountain Historical Company (Chicago: Blakely Printing Company, 1895), 242–47.

28. Certificate no. 7734, issued to Joseph F. Prinster, January 20, 1896, reception no. 590, recorded in volume 15A, page 333, Records of the Clerk and Recorder, Otero County, Colorado.

29. Water deed, Otero Canal Company, to Joseph F. Prinster, January 26, 1892, reception no. 3366, Book 10, page 18; Ditch Statement, reception no. 3604, July 12, 1894, receipt no. 7734, Records of the Clerk and Recorder, Otero County, Colorado.

30. Warranty deed, Henry Heckman to J.F. Prinster, January 17, 1902, reception no. 27789, Book 64, page 416; reception no. 39330, Book 80, page 356, January 1905; reception no. 39485, Book 80, page 392, February 1905.

31. Interview with Brother Nicholas, August 2010; U.S. passport application, 1795–1925, for Bohuslav Kroboth; "List or Manifest of Alien Passengers for the United States," SS *Kronland*, sailing from Antwerp, October 1, 1911; letter from Brother Nicholas to Anthony Prinster, October 8, 2010.

32. *La Junta Tribune*, March 16, 1898; August 22, 1900; March 19, 1902; May 3, 1902; May 14, 1902.

33. Interviews with Joseph C. Prinster, September 17, 2008; January 15, 2009; January 28, 2009.
34. *La Junta Tribune*, May 30, 1908.
35. Letter from Joseph to family, 1909.
36. *La Junta Tribune*, May 20, 1916.
37. Recounted by Ann Griffin, based on conversations with her mother, Josephine Prinster DeOnier.
38. Warranty deed, James McNeen to Millie Prinster, October 16, 1920, reception no. 133715, Book 216, page 407, Records of the Clerk and Recorder, Otero County, Colorado; *Daily Democrat*, June 3, 1922.
39. Interviews with John H. Prinster, June 6, 2012, and August 30, 2012. Information for this chapter as well as other parts of the book was supplied through personal interviews with and statements from John H. Prinster. Twelve such interviews with John and both authors took place between June 6, 2012, and June 24, 2013. Recordings of these interviews are preserved and available.
40. Laurena Maynes Davis, article in *Express Lines* 4, issue no. 3 (March 1999).
41. *Daily Democrat*, September 21, 1922; September 23, 1922; July 31, 1923.
42. *La Junta Tribune*, 1923.
43. *Daily Democrat*, August 11, 1924.
44. Handwritten note from the Mary Blevins files. The note is undated, unsigned and written in pen and ink. Document is in author's files designated exhibit no. 24.
45. *Daily Democrat*, December 23, 1935.
46. *Daily Democrat*, January 11, 1939; January 19, 1939; State of Colorado, Bureau of Vital Statistics, death certificate of Millie F. Prinster; interview with Miriam Peckham, February 22, 2009.
47. Interviews with Miriam Peckham, February 22, 2009, and March 12, 2009; memorial letter, Miriam Peckham, January 1, 2005; *La Junta Tribune-Democrat*, various articles.

PART II

48. Essay about Paul Henry Prinster, undated and unsigned, found in scrapbook kept by Josephine Patterson Prinster.
49. Marriage license of Paul H. Prinster and Carrie A. Palmer, April 12, 1916, marriage license records, document no. 2534, page 263, Records of the Clerk and Recorder, Otero County, Colorado; *La Junta Tribune*, April 27, 1912.
50. State of Colorado, Bureau of Vital Statistics, death certificate of Carrie A. Prinster, registered no. 28, May 12, 1916; *La Junta Tribune*, May 13, 1916; May 20, 1916.
51. *Daily Sentinel*, "Story of Prinster Brothers Typical."
52. Interview with Joseph C. Prinster, January 28, 2009.
53. Marriage license of Paul H. Prinster and Edna May Lampson, August 19, 1919, document no. 4101 (L), page 148, Records of the Clerk and Recorder, Otero County, Colorado.
54. *Daily Sentinel*, "Story of Prinster Brothers Typical."
55. *Daily Sentinel*, "Grand Junction Twenty Years Ago Today," Saturday, March 6, 1920.
56. *Daily Democrat*, September 19, 1921; July 31, 1923.

57. Interviews with John H. Prinster.
58. Frank J. Prinster Jr., "History of City Market," March 8, 1994, unpublished article, document is in author's files designated exhibit no. 34.
59. *Daily Sentinel*, April 30, 1924.
60. Letter from Joseph A. Booker to Anthony F. Prinster, January 27, 1999. Joseph Booker is the grandson of Adam Booker.
61. Interviews with John H. Prinster.
62. Memories of Frank Prinster Sr., as told to Anthony Prinster.
63. Brother Nicholas, "Grandma Jody's Special Talents," written for the children, grandchildren and great-grandchildren of Frank and Josephine Prinster on the occasion of the family reunion held July 1996 in Grand Junction, Colorado.
64. Letter from Brother Nicholas to Tony Prinster, October 8, 2012.
65. Marriage license of Frank J. Prinster and Josephine Patterson, June 22, 1914, Records of the Clerk and Recorder, Otero County, Colorado.
66. U.S. passport applications, 1795–1925, records for Frank J. Prinster and Leo G. Prinster.
67. Interviews with Joseph C. Prinster, January 28 and 29, 2009.
68. Interview with Joseph C. Prinster; conversations with Frank Prinster Jr.; memories related by Ann Griffin.
69. Ann Griffin's account of conversations with her mother.
70. Brother Nicholas, "Grandma Jody's Special Talents"; letter from Brother Nicholas to Anthony F. Prinster, October 8, 2010.
71. Ann Griffin's account of conversations with her mother, Josephine Prinster DeOnier.
72. Interviews with Joseph C. Prinster.
73. Margie Prinster, "Mr. Prinster Goes to Lunch," unpublished essay written in 1944 or 1945.
74. Teo Prinster, "F.J.P.," essay written in 1996; interview with Teo Prinster by Ann Griffin, November 1994; letter from Cliff Baldridge to Frank, Joe and Teo Prinster, December 28, 1975.
75. Letter from Cliff Baldridge to Frank, Joe and Teo Prinster, December 28, 1975.
76. Conversation with Father Edward Prinster, circa 1954.
77. Miriam Blevins's account, as told to her by her mother, Mary Prinster Blevins.
78. History of City Market, March 8, 1994; interviews with John H. Prinster, August 2012.
79. Otero County Directory, 1919.
80. Interview with Teo Prinster by Ann Griffin, November 1994.
81. *Daily Sentinel*, June 29, 1932.
82. Interviews with Patricia "Penny" Prinster.
83. Interviews with John H. Prinster; *Express Lines* 4, issue no. 4 (April 1999).
84. Interviews with Patricia "Penny" Prinster.
85. *Daily Sentinel*, August 1950.
86. Interviews with Fran Wilson Higgins, the niece of Clarence Prinster.
87. Interviews with John H. Prinster.
88. Warranty deed, November 14, 1939, reception no. 359973, Book 387, page 7, Records of the Clerk and Recorder, Mesa County, Colorado.
89. Interview with John H. Prinster.
90. The Art Center, Western Colorado Center for the Arts, permanent collection.

91. *Denver Catholic Register*, May 20, 1937.
92. *Denver Catholic Register*, April 23, 1939.
93. *Steamboat Pilot*, December 5, 1940.
94. YampaValley, "Wadge Mine Explosion 1942," yampavalley.info, http://yampavalley.info/centers/history_%2526_genealogy/pages/mining/pages/wadge_mine_explosion_1942; GenDisasters, "Mount Harris, CO Explosion in Victor American Mine, Jan 1942," http://www3.gendisasters.com/colorado/5638/mount-harris-explosion-victor-american-mine-jan-1942.
95. *Denver Catholic Register*, December 12, 1956.
96. *Steamboat Pilot*, December 12, 1956.

PART III

97. Pasquale Marranzino, "Early Colorado Grocery Family," *Rocky Mountain News*, November 1964.
98. Deed to Freda Prinster, Book 280, page 457, Records of the Clerk and Recorder, Mesa County, Colorado; deed to Goldie Prinster, Book 279, page 253, Records of the Clerk and Recorder, Mesa County, Colorado; deed to Josephine A. Prinster, Book 280, page 266, Records of the Clerk and Recorder, Mesa County, Colorado.
99. Letter from Joseph A. Booker to Anthony F. Prinster, January 27, 1999; *Daily Sentinel*, October 11, 1939.
100. Interview with Joseph C. Prinster; interview with Teo Prinster by Ann Griffin, November 1994.
101. Interview with Joseph C. Prinster; Prinster family history, June 30, 2011; *Express Lines* 4, issue no. 4 (April 1999).
102. Deed to Josephine Alice Prinster, grantee, Book 356, page 223, Records of the Clerk and Recorder, Mesa County, Colorado.
103. Interview with Joseph C. Prinster.
104. Pearl E. Warren to Leo G. Prinster et al., reception no. 343374, Records of the Clerk and Recorder, Mesa County, Colorado; Biggs-Kurtz Investment Company, a Corporation, to Leo G. Prinster et al., reception no. 346165, Records of the Clerk and Recorder, Mesa County, Colorado.
105. *Grocer's Digest*, May 1940.
106. Warranty deed, November 14, 1939, reception no. 359973, Book 387, page 7, Records of the Clerk and Recorder, Mesa County, Colorado.
107. *Express Lines* 4, issue no. 5 (May 1999).
108. Interview with Joseph C. Prinster; financial journals of Frank J. Prinster Sr., January 1, 1936–January 1, 1958.
109. *Daily Sentinel*, October 11, 1939.
110. *Grocer's Digest*, May 1940.
111. *Daily Sentinel*, October 11, 1939.
112. Interview with John H. Prinster.
113. Prinster family history, June 30, 2011.

114. Cathy White, "The First Person" (column), "Modest Example; Average Man," *Montrose Daily Press*, November 1, 1995.
115. History of City Market, Frank J. Prinster Jr., March 8, 1994.
116. CS Morey Mercantile Building, story site no. 311, Historic Denver Inc., created by Denver Storytrek.
117. Telephone interview by Laurena Mayne Davis with Katie Bristol, November 1998.
118. *Express Lines* 4, issue no. 6 (June 1999).
119. Raymond W. Taylor and Samuel W. Taylor, *Uranium Fever, or No Talk Under $1 Million* (New York: Macmillan Company, 1970).
120. *Express Lines* 4, issue no. 6.
121. *Denver Post*, December 14, 1955.
122. Sunday Edition, circa 1943–44, "Prinster Brothers Open New Market for Montrose District." Possibly from the *Montrose Daily Press*, but neither the name of the paper nor the exact date can be determined; document is in author's files designated exhibit no. 55.
123. Warranty deed from Leo G. Prinster, Paul H. Prinster and Frank J. Prinster, grantors, to Leo G. Prinster, Paul H. Prinster, Frank J. Prinster, Clarence F. Prinster, Frank J. Prinster Jr. and Paul C. Prinster Jr., grantees, November 20, 1939, reception no. 359973, Records of the Clerk and Recorder, Mesa County, Colorado.
124. State of Colorado, Department of State certificates for Prinster Brothers Inc., document no. 19541127507; Colorado Wholesale Grocers Inc., document no. 19541127508; North Avenue City Market Inc., document no. 195411227510; City Market Inc., document no. 19871213908.
125. Lease agreement, Cortez City Market, June 25, 1967, Amended Certificate of Limited Partnership, Cortez City Market; lease agreement, Durango City Market, June 25, 1967, Amended Certificate of Limited Partnership, Durango City Market; lease agreement, Glenwood City Market, June 25, 1967, Amended Certificate of Limited Partnership, Glenwood City Market; lease agreement, Montrose City Market, June 25, 1967, Amended Certificate of Limited Partnership, Montrose City Market.
126. Interview with Curt Robinson, April 29, 2013.
127. First National Bank in Grand Junction, Registrar of the Debenture Issue; letter from D.J. Vogel to debenture holders, October 7, 1967.
128. Interview with Curt Robinson, April 29, 2013.
129. *The American Catholic Who's Who*, vol. 5, "T. Raber Taylor" (N.p., n.d.), 430.
130. Interview with John H. Prinster.
131. In the Matter of the Estate of Paul H. Prinster in the County Court, Mesa County, Colorado, May 8, 1957, Decree of Final Settlement.
132. Interview with Curt Robinson.
133. Joseph C. Prinster, presentation to Museum of Mesa County, circa 2003, CD/Video.
134. Interview with Curt Robinson, April 30, 2013; Joseph C. Prinster, presentation to Museum of Mesa County.
135. Interview with Joseph C. Prinster.
136. Ibid.
137. Interviews with Curt Robinson.
138. Interviews with John H. Prinster.

139. Interview with Joseph C. Prinster; Joseph C. Prinster, presentation to Museum of Mesa County.
140. Interview with Herb Bacon.
141. Interview with Joseph C. Prinster, Joseph C. Prinster, presentation to Museum of Mesa County.
142. Interview with Joseph C. Prinster.
143. Ibid.
144. Marranzino, "Early Colorado Grocery Family."
145. *Denver Law Journal* 58, no. 6, "In Memoriam" (1980–81).
146. *Express Lines* 4, issue no. 10 (October 1999).
147. Interview with Dick McMillen, March 9, 2013.
148. *Express Lines* 4, issue no. 8 (August 1999).
149. Interview with Curt Robinson, April 19, 2013.
150. State of Colorado, Department of State certificates for Prinster Brothers Inc., document no. 19541127507; Colorado Wholesale Grocers Inc., document no. 19541127508; North Avenue City Market Inc., document no. 195411227510; City Market Inc., document no. 19871213908.
151. *Express Lines* 4, issue no. 8 (August 1999).
152. Interview with Curt Robinson, April 19, 2013.
153. Interview with Joseph C. Prinster.
154. Ibid.
155. Ibid.
156. State of Colorado, Department of State certificates for Prinster Brothers Inc., document no. 19541127507; Colorado Wholesale Grocers Inc., document no. 19541127508; North Avenue City Market Inc., document no. 195411227510; City Market Inc., document no. 19871213908.
157. Interview with Curt Robinson, April 19, 2013
158. Ibid.
159. Interview with John H. Prinster, June 24, 2013.
160. Laurena Maynes Davis, article in *Express Lines* 4, issue no. 7 (July 1999).
161. Laurena Maynes Davis, "Frank Prinster Dies at Age 81," *Daily Sentinel*, July 1996; George Orbanek, editorial, "Frank Prinster," *Daily Sentinel*, July 1996; *Daily Sentinel*, "Mass for Former City Market President Planned Monday," July 1996; handwritten letter from Leo T. (Teo) Prinster to Frank Prinster, June 28, 1996.
162. Interview with Joe C. Prinster, September 17, 2008.
163. Ibid.
164. Joseph C. Prinster, presentation to Museum of Mesa County.
165. Laurena Maynes Davis, article in *Express Lines* 4, issue no. 11 (November 1999).
166. *Daily Sentinel*, obituary for Leo T. Prinster, August 10, 2012; *Express Lines* 4, issue no. 12 (December 1999).
167. Letter from Teo to Frank, June 28, 1996.
168. *Daily Sentinel*, obituary for Leo T. Prinster.
169. Laurena Maynes Davis, article in *Express Lines* 4, issue no. 12 (December 1999); interview with Phyllis Norris, May 23, 2013.

170. City Market Inc., Grand Junction, Colorado, financial statements and store and department operating statements for the thirteen weeks ending on January 1, 1994.

171. Amy Erickson, "The Concept of One Stop Shopping Prevails," *Vail Daily*, May 21, 1997.

INDEX

J

K

L

M

N

O

P

R

S

T

U

V

W

Y

Z

ABOUT THE AUTHORS

ANTHONY F. PRINSTER (Tony) is the great-grandson of Josef Pruenster, whose sons are "the Brothers Four." The author holds a BA from the University of Notre Dame and a JD from the University of Colorado. He is of Counsel with the law firm Hoskin Farina & Kampf in Grand Junction, Colorado. Tony and the Prinster family are respected civic leaders in western Colorado.

KATE RULAND-THORNE is a regular contributor of local history stories for *Grand Valley Magazine*. Her feature stories also have appeared in *Arizona Highways* and *Southwest Art* magazines. Kate was editor of *Sedona* magazine and has written seven regional history books, including *Lion of Redstone*, published by Johnson Publishing. She holds a BA degree from Southern Methodist University.